Carolyn Vella and John McGonagle

Burmese Cats

Everything About Acquisition, Care, Nutrition,
Behavior, Health Care, and Breeding

With 40 Color Photographs

Illustrations by Michele Earle-Bridges

Dedication

This book is dedicated to Kay Mowers, owner of Waterford Cattery, a dedicated and responsible breeder of Burmese cats. Thanks for all your help with this book and for the opportunity to handle and appreciate North American Winner, Supreme Grand Champion Waterford's Lonedoux. The Fancy will miss you, Kay, but you live on through the beauty and perfection of your Burmese cats.

© Copyright 1995 by Barron's Educational Series, Inc.

All inquiries should be addressed to:
Barron's Educational Series, Inc.
250 Wireless Boulevard
Hauppauge, NY 11788

International Standard Book No. 0-8120-9158-2

Library of Congress Catalog Card No. 95-41969

Library of Congress Cataloging-in-Publication Data

Vella, Carolyn M.
    Burmese cats : everything about acquisition, care, nutrition, behavior, health care, and breeding / Carolyn Vella, John McGonagle.
        p.   cm.—(A Complete pet owner's manual)
    Includes bibliographical references (p.   ) and index.
    ISBN 0-8120-9158-2
    1. Burmese cat. I. McGonagle, John J. II. Title. III. Series.
SF449.B8V45   1995
636.8´25—dc20   95-41969
                                                            CIP

Printed in Hong Kong

5678   9955   987654321

About the Authors

Carolyn Vella is a member of the Board of Directors of the Cat Writers' Association and a judge with the American Association of Cat Enthusiasts, Inc. (AACE). She is the author of numerous articles on cats, cat collectibles, and showing cats in publications ranging from *Devon Rex!, B.O.B.S.* (Breeders of Bobtails Society), and *Animal Talk* to *National Cat (Australia), Cat World™ International,* and *Cat Collectors.*

John McGonagle is a former president of the AACE, a judge with AACE, and a professional member of the Cat Writers' Association. He has written articles on cats and cat-related subjects for *Cats, B.O.B.S., The TICA Yearbook, Popular Cats* and *Cat World™ International.*

Carolyn and John are co-owners of Jacat Cattery, which breeds Japanese Bobtail and Japanese Bobtail Longhair cats. Their cats have achieved grand championships in four different cat associations. They are the coauthors of *In the Spotlight: A Guide to Showing Pedigreed and Household Pet Cats* (1990) and have co-written articles for *Cat Fancy* and *Cats USA.*

While not breeders of Burmese, they have had the pleasure of assisting Burmese breeders in delivering and caring for Burmese kittens.

Photo Credits:

Chanan: inside back cover, pages 4, 13, 17, 37, 44, 49, 53, 56 (bottom), 60, 64, 68, 73, 77, 80, 81, 88; Donna J. Coss: inside front cover, pages 25, 52, 56 (top), 76; Susan Green: pages 29, 32, 40, 45; Jane Howard: pages 9, 12, 21, 69, 72; Larry Johnson: pages 8, 20, 48, 65; Bob Schwartz: front cover, back cover, pages 16, 24, 33, 41 (top and bottom), 61, 84.

Contents

Four recognized Burmese colors: sable, blue, champagne, and platinum.

Preface

We have written this book for anyone who either wants to buy a Burmese or already owns one. Feel free to dip into it as well as read it from cover to cover. We have tried to make it a useful and interesting resource. In general, we have written this as if we were all sitting down together, talking about your new kitten or answering your questions about what is involved in buying a Burmese. To the extent we could, we have used as little technical material as possible, but in areas such as genetics and breeding it is really unavoidable. We trust that we have not sacrificed accuracy to readability.

At some points, we suggest that you talk with your veterinarian or check current books for additional help on a particular subject, as cat care and cat medicine is always changing. The best way to be a good owner is to keep current.

Throughout this book, we have sometimes referred to your Burmese as "him" or "he," and sometimes to "her" and "she." We try to avoid calling a specific cat of any breed "it." Whatever the sex, we are sure you will love and treasure your Burmese.

Acknowledgments

No book is written without both help and research. We would like to thank the following for their time, expertise, and contributions to writing this book: AACE All-breed cat judge and Burmese breeder Edd Toepelman for access to his records, to out-of-print materials, and to his pictures as well as for his advice; Terry W. Stanglein, V.M.D. for his expert veterinary advice; the Burmese Breed Section of AACE, which responded to our request to all cat registries for input to this book; RASCC (Australia) All-breed cat judge Bambi-Joy Edwards of Bajimbi Cattery for photographs of her winning Burmese of many colors; Larry C. Emmans-Jelinek of Gingerhill Cattery (Canada) for his information on the Mahajaya import line of Burmese; and Ann L. Graham and Peggy Hawkins for providing pictures of their beautiful Burmese.

Portions of the chapter on showing are adapted with permission from the American Association of Cat Enthusiasts, Inc.'s "Helpful Hints for the New Exhibitor," 1993. The chart in the chapter on breeding is adapted with permission from the Reading-Berks Coalition of Responsible Dog and Cat Fanciers, "Should You Breed Your Pet?" (1994).

Introduction to the Burmese Cat

This book presents to you one of the most beautiful of the purebred cats in the Fancy (term used to denote the community of breeders of purebred cats and exhibitors of purebred and household pet cats), the Burmese. We will introduce you to the Burmese, his appearance and temperament, and will help you to find, and then lovingly care for, the Burmese you acquire.

Even though this book is about Burmese, some of you may not have yet made up your mind about whether or not a Burmese is the cat for you, or even if you should get a cat at all. The

The Burmese's moderate body is just one of a variety of body types of domestic cats. Other types range from long and tubular to stocky or "cobby."

decision about how you choose a new cat is an important one. Before you go further, let us help you understand more about this process.

Let us say you've already decided you want a cat. How did that happen? More than likely, you just fell in love with a particular cat. His owner told you he was a purebred (or perhaps he or she said he was a "registered") cat. Now you want a registered or "show" cat. Perhaps you want a cat just like the one you saw. But you may not want that breed—you may want a cat of another breed. What do you do?

First, you should realize that every recognized purebred in the Fancy is unique. There are medium-sized breeds that are heavy, sturdy, and muscular cats. There are dainty, small-boned, slender cats. There are moderate-sized cats with unique ears or tails. There are large cats that originally made the northern forests of the world their domain. There are cats with coats that are fluffy, tight, silky, shaggy, curly, or even almost nonexistent. Purebred cats come in every color of the rainbow and their coat patterns range from a solid color to multicolored. If you like a certain appearance in your pet, you can find what you like in a purebred cat.

But before you decide on a cat, you owe it to yourself to understand what life is like with a cat.

Life with a Cat

Even though you may not yet have selected your breed, we'll talk as if you have chosen a Burmese. Life with a Burmese is a very special experience. As a kitten, your little bundle of fur and legs will keep you laughing as he plays and pounces, acting out the lives of both a sweet and somewhat helpless baby and a big, ferocious, fearless tiger in the jungle.

As your kitten grows into a cat, you will have the wonderful opportunity of sharing all the experiences of his life and all his adventures. You will share his surprise at discovering all the things he is able to do as he gets bigger in size. Celebrating your holidays will take on a whole new dimension by sharing them with a cat.

As your Burmese gets older and settles down, you will experience the true, uncompromising friendship with an animal—a friend who will love you no matter what, a friend you can talk to, cry to, and laugh with. No matter what your mood, he is there for you. He will be a true companion in every sense of the word. The relationship of human and cat is one of the most delightful, wonderful, special relationships that exists.

But with those delights come responsibilities.

Your Responsibility to Your Burmese

Before you decide to buy your Burmese, or any other breed of cat, you should recognize that being a Burmese owner carries with it a significant level of responsibility. Above all, you will want to keep your cat safe. First and foremost, you must keep your Burmese indoors. While there are no hard statistics, our experience and that of practicing veterinarians indicates that the lifespan of an indoor cat is several times that of the outdoor cat. Even the occasional time spent outside exposes your Burmese to risks that are not present inside: such as cars and other vehicles, free-roaming cats (and

Your Burmese will quickly become a member of your family, sharing his attention and affection with everyone.

the diseases they carry), weed-killing chemicals, dogs, and more.

You will want to keep your Burmese healthy over his life (which now can be up to 20 years). That means altering your pet as soon as you and your veterinarian agree that you can, maintaining proper nutrition for all stages of his life, and seeing your veterinarian for vaccinations and regular preventative health care. You will want to keep your cat (and you) happy, which means allowing time for you to play and socialize with him.

Cats like their environment clean, just as we do, so daily care of the litter box is critical. For someone who has never owned a cat, this may seem excessive, particularly when you are confronted with ads for litters that "eliminate" odors. One of the leading reasons cats have accidents outside of a litter box is actually due to dirty litter boxes. Remember, a Burmese's sense of smell is much more sensitive than ours, so a box that seems clean and odor-free to you may not be clean to your cat. In fact, it may have an

Sable male and female.

offensive odor. And even the best litter-trained cat will avoid a dirty litter box.

While Burmese are clean themselves (in fact they will wash themselves every day), regular grooming with a brush helps to pull the dead fur out of their coat. That, in turn, helps to prevent hair balls. Even a shorthaired cat like a Burmese can have hair balls, particularly in the spring. In addition, brushing your Burmese's coat is an enjoyable activity for you. Some researchers have even told us that the very act of brushing a cat and feeling it purr is as relaxing for the owner as it is for the cat.

While Burmese cats will be quite content to play at home while you're away at work, they are not meant to be left alone while you are away for an extended period of time. And every day you must:

1. Remove old food and give your cat fresh food and water.

2. Clean the litter box.

3. Play with and cuddle your cat.

If you have to be away from home for an extended period of time, you can make sure your Burmese is properly cared for in several ways:

• You can put your cat in a boarding facility while you are away.

• You can have a reliable, experienced friend stop by each day to take care of these chores.

• You can pay a pet sitting service to come into your home to care for your Burmese (see Interviewing Pet Sitters, page 40).

These responsibilities are easily handled—and they are so little to give in exchange for the years of love you will experience from your beautiful Burmese.

What Does "Registered" Mean?

If you are going to buy a Burmese, that really means you are buying a

Champagne Burmese female.

purebred cat, and that, in turn means you are buying a "registered" cat. It sounds complicated, but it is not.

A registered cat is one whose litter has been registered with one of the cat registry associations, such as the American Association of Cat Enthusiasts (AACE) or the Cat Fanciers' Association (CFA). (See United States Cat Registries, page 95.) A litter of kittens can be registered only if both the queen (the kittens' mother) and the sire (the father of the kittens) are already registered and the litter meets certain technical qualifications. These include requirements that the parents be of a certain breed, that the papers be signed by the owners of the queen and sire, and that all of the kittens be described according to sex, color, and pattern.

Technically speaking, if a Burmese is not registered, it really cannot be considered a purebred. (In fact, in Canada, this is the law.) That is because you cannot be certain about the breed of the parents without relying on the registration process.

So, if a cat is called a purebred but is not registered, and it looks like a Burmese, what you actually have is a cat that only *appears* to be a Burmese—you cannot be certain that it is one. This means that when you see a purebred Burmese for sale at a pet store, don't assume that it is a registered Burmese. And, if you see a "registered" Burmese at a pet store, please don't assume it is also a show-quality Burmese. A show-quality Burmese is something different, as we will explain later.

Choosing a Breed

If you have already decided on a Burmese, you do not need to worry about choosing from among the many wonderful breeds of cats. But, if you have not yet made up your mind, read on.

When deciding on the right breed for you, a good way to get a sense of what makes each breed special is to read the breed profiles that are published in the various cat magazines.

They should give you a common basis on which to compare the many varieties of purebred cats.

If you do not have access to the back issues of the cat magazines, or cannot wait for the next breed profile to be published, then read one of the many fine books that describe the various breeds of purebred cats. We have included the name of one of these by Gloria Stephens on page 95. It may be found in your library. The photos of the different breeds are beautiful, and, with the text, will help you capture the essence of many of the breeds. If you cannot find this one, try to find a similar book, but try to stay with one that is relatively current and that features pictures from the United States. Over time, the look of cats has gradually changed, so you will want to see how they look today. Also, Burmese (and other breeds) in other countries may look different from those in the United States.

Cat Shows

If you want to see the various breeds in person, you should attend a cat show. You can find out where they are by looking at the show calendars in the back of the various cat magazines. When you are at the cat show, look at the cats as well as the kittens, both in the judging rings and in their show cages. After you have looked around, talk with the breeders of the breeds in which you are interested. Tell the breeders how you live, and what you are seeking. Most will be very helpful about how their breed fits your lifestyle. While each kitten is an individual, your kitten will tend to have a personality similar to those of others of its breed, so this can be very helpful.

If you and your cat have very different personalities, and if these personalities cannot adapt to each other, your relationship with your cat will not be a happy one. For example, if you have a very active environment, you want to make certain you don't select a breed that is basically shy. A high activity level can upset some breeds, while a quiet environment is not stimulating enough for other breeds.

In considering what breed is for you, answer the following questions. Do you have children? Do you have another cat or a dog? Are you looking for a lap cat or a more lively breed? The answers can make a difference in which breed you select.

In turn, you should feel free to ask the breeders your own questions:
• How big will this breed of cat get when it is fully grown?
• What types of food does it eat, and how often should it eat?
• How much, and what kind of grooming or other care does it need?
• Does it need the companionship of another cat, another animal, or a person?
• Is there any difference in the disposition of the males and the females? (There often is, but, contrary to what you might expect, sometimes the males make better, sweeter companions.)

Also, if possible, get references. Just ask to talk with some people to whom the breeders have sold kittens in the past. They can give you the best idea of what it is like to live with that breed and with that breeder's kittens.

What Is a Burmese?

History of the Burmese

While sometimes (incorrectly) called a "plain brown cat," the Burmese has had anything but a plain history. As a breed, its history is intertwined with that of at least three other breeds: the Siamese, the Tonkinese, and the Bombay. The Burmese breed history also includes within it a "temporary" breed, the Malayan.

In the United States, the history of the Burmese begins with the arrival in the 1930s of Wong Mau, a female cat. From then on, many elements of the development of the breed in the United States are subject to differences of opinion and even controversy.

According to some reports, Wong Mau was brought into the United States by Dr. Joseph Thompson, a psychiatrist. Other reports indicate that Wong Mau was actually acquired by Thompson only after coming to the United States. The generally accepted history from that point has it that Dr. Thompson saw Wong Mau, a walnut brown cat with darker points (tips of the ears and tail), as not merely a dark Siamese cat but rather as a different breed. Critics of Thompson's theory argued that Wong Mau was just a "bad Siamese."

To keep this new breed going, Wong Mau was bred to a Sealpoint Siamese cat, the cat closest to Wong Mau's type. Dr. Thompson evidently believed that breeding to a cat with the seal color (a brown/black color) that originated from the same part of the world—the Malay peninsula—was the best he could do. Unfortunately, the cats resulting from this breeding were even less impressive to the Fancy than Wong Mau herself.

To demonstrate the existence of the new breed he saw exemplified by Wong Mau, Thompson undertook a complex series of breedings. These involved outcrosses to Siamese and then inbreeding to the resulting cats. (See Glossary, page 93 for an explanation of these terms.) (The method used and the complex series of resulting relationships is of interest only to geneticists.) The results, Thompson argued, showed that Wong Mau was carrying elements of both a new breed, which he called the "Burmese," as well as of an already-recognized breed, the Siamese. The name Burmese was chosen to associate the cat with what Thompson believed to be its area of origin, Burma (now Myanmar) on the Malay peninsula.

Historians and geneticists now contend that Wong Mau was either a Burmese-Siamese variant or a true Tonkinese cat (described later), which is today seen as the descendant of a Burmese-Siamese cross. To confuse things even more, according to the late Don Shaw, a cat show judge and geneticist, a review of the photos of this first Burmese showed that she was a true "pointed" cat.

Dr. Thompson's efforts actually initiated what some believe was the first time in cat Fancy history that specific breeding experiments were designed and carried out to define the genetics of a potential new breed. In fact, in the 1930s, the Siamese and Burmese were quite similar in appearance (called conformation), so that the experiments were aimed at showing

Sable Burmese female with beautiful eyes.

that these were actually quite different breeds.

In spite of this program to breed Burmese to Siamese, two additional Burmese were imported in 1941. They were shipped from Burma to the United States in December, 1941, just as the war in the Pacific came to their former home on the Malay peninsula. (Only one of these has left descendants.) Following World War II, activity in breeding Burmese in the United States picked up its pace.

Regardless of the true genetic make-up of Wong Mau, the Burmese as a breed has had one of the more unusual histories in the Fancy. Currently, the Burmese, at least in the traditional sable color (a brown), is recognized for competition by every U.S. cat registry. That is the only traditional element of its recent history.

Picking up the thread of the history of the Burmese, after its arrival in the United States, the Burmese cat was accepted for competition by several United States registries, including the Cat Fanciers' Association (CFA), the country's largest registry.

However, its acceptance there was short lived.

Approval Withdrawn

By the late 1940s, CFA had withdrawn its approval of Burmese to be shown, or even registered with it. There were evidently several reasons for this. Some people pointed out that the Burmese appeared to be kept alive as a breed only by regular outcrosses to Siamese. Opponents of the Burmese felt this showed that the Burmese was not really a breed, since it could not breed true. Burmese supporters argued that they did this only because the Burmese gene pool was so small. They argued that if outcrosses to Siamese had not been allowed, the result would have been extreme inbreeding of the few existing Burmese. Regardless of which side was correct, while the use of the outcrosses kept the breed from vanishing, it did mean that the Burmese might never be a breed of its own since its continued existence then depended on Burmese owners being able to breed their cats to cats of another recognized breed on a regular basis.

Another reason often given for the withdrawal relates to the position of the Siamese cat breeders, who made up a large and important part of the Fancy at that time. This point of view asserts that the Siamese breeders objected both to the use of Siamese in the Burmese breeding program, as well as to the initial acceptance of a cat that they regarded as being "half" Siamese.

Whatever the reason or reasons, the Burmese had its certification in CFA removed in 1947. In spite of this (or perhaps because of it), the Burmese breeders then began to work on the breed to distinguish it from its relative, the Siamese cat. They worked to "weed out" cats with show faults, such as kinks in the tails, or lockets (white markings in the neck

A handsome blue Burmese.

area).This was done by altering cats that showed such faults to avoid a breeding that would pass them along to a new generation of cats.

In addition, some of the breeders tried to eliminate what they saw as Siamese-looking cats (in terms of head type, as well as those with light colors) from their breeding programs. At the same time, they worked to produce cats whose pedigrees showed only Burmese cats, with no Siamese cats at all, for at least three generations back.

This hard work eventually paid off. Certification by CFA was re-granted for the sable Burmese 10 years later, in 1957. From there on, the number of Burmese catteries and Burmese cats began to show a steady increase.

Colored Cats

Then, in 1974, several Burmese were imported from the Mahajaya Cattery in Thailand. They were also known as the "Thai Copper Cats." These beautiful Burmese cats are still in breeding programs today, enhancing the small gene pool of the Burmese. However, all during this time, the "plain brown" cat was producing some kittens that were anything but brown: blue (gray), champagne (honey-beige), platinum (silvery-gray), and others. For years, these kittens were treated in one of two radically different ways: some placed as pets with the restriction that they not be bred, or even registered; others sold as a rare mutation (even though they could not be shown).

Some Burmese breeders began to work to secure recognition for these colored cats, known as dilutes, in the U.S. cat registries. Again, the history in CFA takes an odd turn. Most of the breeders of sable Burmese objected to permitting Burmese lines to include these new colors. Burmese were, by their definition, sable. And if the cat was not sable, it could not be a Burmese.

The solution—at least for a while—was to create a new breed, the Malayan. This was essentially a Burmese, but in colors other than sable. So, at least in CFA, a Burmese sire and a Burmese queen could produce two kinds of breeds of kittens, one a (sable) Burmese, and one a (champagne) Malayan.

This odd situation was eventually corrected. In the mid-1980s, the dilute Burmese were finally recognized by CFA as Burmese, as the other U.S. cat registries had already done. But, given the Burmese's history, it should come as no surprise that the various U.S. registries can differ as to *which* colors are acceptable and whether or not Burmese can officially come in the tortoiseshell pattern (mingled red and black) in addition to the accepted solid colors. Exactly which colors and patterns are officially accepted depends upon which registry is involved.

A New Look

Controversy and the Burmese continue to travel together. Over the past decade, a new Burmese look has emerged. One group of Burmese has retained its older look, and is now often called "traditional." Others, bred to produce significantly rounder heads but almost flat faces, are now often called "contemporary" Burmese. The breeders of each look have argued that theirs is really the true Burmese. The result today is that both looks actually exist side by side. It is generally believed by the Burmese breeders that judges in some U.S. cat registries favor the contemporary look; and others favor the traditional look (see the illustration on page 15).

Two Other Breeds

Regardless of issues such as colors and look, the Burmese as a breed has had other important impacts on the cat Fancy. The Burmese is one of the foundation breeds for two other registered breeds: the Tonkinese and the Bombay.

The Tonkinese of today is seen as a merging of the Burmese and Siamese. Its body is mid-way between these two breeds. It comes in a variety of colors (including blue, champagne, platinum) and can have both solid and pointed patterns.

The Bombay was created by breeding the Burmese to a black American Shorthair cat. The result is a man-made breed that has often been described, inaccurately, as a black Burmese.

As if the history of the Burmese breed were not convoluted enough, some cat breeders are now seeking to secure recognition in the various U.S. registries for a cat variously called the Tiffany or the Chantilly. This is a cat that had been described as a longhaired Burmese in the past. Its origins are, not surprisingly, somewhat clouded and, as with the Burmese itself, controversial. Most breeders of this cat now contend that it is not really a longhaired Burmese and, in fact, genetically it has nothing to do with Burmese. And so it goes.

Genetics

Note: Since this book is not meant to be a technical book on the genetics of the Burmese, we have tried to keep this portion of the book as simplified as possible. For those who care to study the genetics of the Burmese in more depth, we refer you to some of the books listed in Useful Addresses and Literature, page 95. The genetics of cats and of cat breeds is still a science in development.

What makes your Burmese a Burmese is his genetic structure. The chromosomes that are responsible for creating your Burmese are themselves made up of thousands of genes. These genes multiply rapidly making identical copies of themselves. However, sometimes when a gene is copying itself, the copy created is not exact. That gene is then considered to have mutated. When this happens, the inexact copies are known as alleles. It is these mutated genes, or alleles, that are the reason for the various colors and types of coat found on the various breeds of cat.

One of these series of alleles is known as the "albino alleles." The albino alleles affect coat color and are responsible for some of the most beautiful breeds of cats in the Fancy. The albino alleles do this by inhibiting the expression of the full color. For example, a black coat becomes brown while an orange coat becomes yellow in the presence of these special alleles.

In technical terms, there actually exists a Burmese gene that is a member of the albino series of alleles. This, in turn, causes the coat color of the Burmese to be a dark sepia or seal brown instead of black. This special genetic mix found in the Burmese also enables these cats to be bred with coat colors of a lighter brown, called champagne and a lilac, called platinum. Burmese also come with red and golden red coats, as well as cream, tortoiseshell (red and black mixed), and dilute tortoiseshell (cream and gray).

While Burmese in the cream and tortoiseshell (called "tortie") coat colors are actively bred in Europe, Australia, and New Zealand, they are rarely seen in the United States because some of the cat registry associations do not accept these coat colors for championship competition. So, the most common Burmese coat color you will usually see in the United States remains the sable with the occasional champagne or platinum.

Today's Burmese comes in one of two types, differentiated by the types of heads: the "traditional" (upper left) and the "contemporary" (lower right). Both types are seen at cat shows.

As Burmese breeders continue to develop the variety of colors that it is possible to produce in the Burmese cat, they would be expected to begin to actively campaign to have the various cat registries in the United States accept the Burmese in these colors in the show ring. As these Burmese are then accepted for championship competition, you will begin to see more of them being bred. And that means a wider variety of colors of Burmese becoming available as pets.

Colors

Today, the most commonly recognized Burmese colors that are accepted for registration purposes in the United States are:

- sable (a deep, rich brown);
- champagne (a warm beige tone

In addition, the following additional colors are also accepted by The International Cat Association (TICA):
• cinnamon (warm honey to orange tinged gold);
• fawn (warm taupe or beige);
• red (deep clear, rich red); and
• various colors of tortoiseshell.

Outside the United States, Burmese are bred in many colors, with no one color being preferred over another. Litters born in catteries we have visited in Australia, for example, are real "rainbows" with red, tortoiseshell, cream, and blue all present in the same litter.

Physical Attributes

The standard for a show-quality Burmese is basically the same in most associations. You will find that most breeders of any pedigreed cat, when asked to describe their breed, will fall back on the breed standard of the association in which they show.

This description is based on the AACE breed standard. It describes a show-quality Burmese.

The Burmese is a cat of medium size, but with substantial bone structure. She should feel much heavier than she looks, without being fat. The weight of the Burmese is carried in her bones and muscles, which are all well developed.

The overall look of the Burmese is that of a round cat. Everything about the cat, from paws to eyes to the tips of the ears, are rounded. The Burmese has a sweet expression on her pleasantly round face. The neck is short and well developed. The tail is medium in length. The eyes can be yellow or gold with brilliant color.

The coat is fine and lies close to the body. It feels like satin when you run your hand along it. No matter what color your Burmese is, her coat should be glossy. In a show-quality Burmese, you will see the color of the coat with-

This blue Burmese's tail position reveals his friendliness and curiosity.

shading to pale golden tan on the underside);
• platinum (a rich silver color with fawn undertones and a slightly pinkish cast); and
• blue (medium to slate blue, often with warm fawn tones).

out any darker color at the extremities ("pointing") or any obvious tabby markings. It is the presence of minor factors such as tabby markings or a small patch of white at the neck that typically distinguish a Burmese that can be exhibited in the championship show ring from a Burmese cat that cannot. However, it is the very same changes in the uniformity of color that can make a pet-quality Burmese unique.

The Contemporary versus the Traditional Looks

Originally, the Burmese had a longer nose than you see today, more like that on the Siamese. This is not surprising, since we know that Siamese were used by breeders in the development of the Burmese. Over time, the nose has become shorter, coming in closer to the rest of the head. In all other respects, the cat is round. This look is today considered to be the traditional look.

Although the Burmese breed standard, the written rules against which a cat is judged in a cat show, requires the cat to be round, an attempt has been made by some Burmese breeders to flatten the Burmese face—to bring the nose more into line with the rest of the head, when viewed from the side. This effort has produced a Burmese with a very high, rounded head (or dome) and a face that looks more like the flatter face seen in the show Persian. This is known now as the contemporary look. Both of these looks are being bred today. They are both Burmese. Which look you, as the new owner of a Burmese, prefer is strictly a matter of aesthetics.

Deformities

At the very beginning of the development of the Burmese breed, the defects within the breed were primarily skeletal in nature. Among those skeletal problems, the biggest problem the

A young sable female.

early breeders faced was a tendency toward dwarfism in the kittens. A desire to enhance the smallness of some of these cats resulted in some Burmese having small heads, with their bodies appearing out of proportion to the head size. Breeders consider that these skeletal defects were due primarily to the inbreeding that was deemed necessary at the time in order to establish the Burmese as a breed. This situation was so common that the written standard for the Burmese in the Cat Fanciers' Association actually reflected a desire for smallness. Now, however, this has been changed, so the written standard for the breed no longer supports smallness in this breed.

In the more recent history of the breed, some Burmese breeders have been moving toward cats with a very flat face similar to the face of the Persian (the contemporary look). The movement toward the flatter face was accomplished by selective breeding among a specific pool of Burmese cats chosen to achieve this look. That breeding program caused some genetic problems in some of the kittens born of these flatter-faced parents. Specifically, kittens of such breedings can be born with open skulls or misplaced eyes. These kittens quickly die.

In addition, Burmese kittens, regardless of look, are prone to a disorder of the third eyelid. In that case, the eyelid prolapses (comes out) and reveals the tear duct. This condition is known as "cherry eye" and can be surgically corrected.

While these issues are important to breeders, if you are buying a Burmese for a pet, they will not really directly impact you, because, when you buy a pet from a responsible breeder, you will be dealing with a healthy kitten. You should be aware that:
• no responsible breeder will sell you a kitten that has had corrective eye surgery without telling you this and making certain that you have the veterinary records concerning the procedure; and
• no responsible breeder would ever sell you a kitten to be used in a breed-

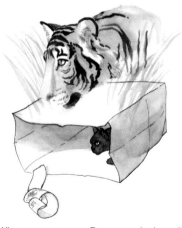

When you see your Burmese playing with a bag, you are also seeing a "tiger in a cave"—or so she sees it.

ing program if he or she knows that the lines of the cat will produce skull deformities and associated problems.

Personality

The Burmese is a very person-oriented cat and will come to you easily. One Burmese historian has said that the "Burmese will turn on the most soulful eyes in catdom and 'con' you out of everything you own." [Rosemonde S. Peltz, M.D., *The Burmese Cat*]

Burmese are quite content to spend their evening in your lap or sitting by your side sharing your evening's relaxation. This is not to say that the Burmese cat is a "couch potato." The breed is very active, especially the kittens. They love to play with their toys and will keep you entertained with their antics. They are highly intelligent cats and easily adapt to your home, in spite of the normal trauma associated with moving or coming to a new home. They typically overcome that very quickly. Once your Burmese knows where her food dish and litter box are (so make sure you show her), she will accept your home as her own. From there, she will find her own special places and gradually adjust to your routine.

People often ask which has the better personality—the male or the female. Your authors have a fundamental disagreement on "boys versus girls" in any breed. Everyone sees what they want in a cat or kitten, just a little differently. What that really means is that personality varies from cat to cat, depending on how they were raised, how you live, what other cats you have, etc. While breeders say that there are some slight differences (altered males are sometimes labeled as "laid back" while females are called "curious"), it is a fact that Burmese, regardless of sex, are not usually shy. There are many stories about them deciding to join you in the bath! They are social and playful, above all.

Buying a Burmese

What Age Cat Do You Want?

It seems to us that everyone wants a kitten, and only a kitten. And it seems that people want to get the kittens as young as possible. That is because we all see kittens as little balls of fur and fun, but, you will soon find that most breeders will not sell you a very young kitten. As a rule, most breeders will not even release a kitten until it is about four months old. There are several reasons for this. First, breeders want to make sure that the kitten is healthy, and has had all of its shots. And, for rabies, for example, veterinarians usually want the kitten to be at least 4 months old to assure that the shot will "take." Also, cats cannot usually be shipped by air if they are under three months old.

To be frank, taking care of a very young kitten is not always as easy—or pleasant—as you might think. It requires a lot of time, experience, dedication, and knowledge. If a kitten is too young, the trauma of moving—and there is trauma—can be considerable.

The last point is an important one, and one that you as a potential buyer of a Burmese kitten should be aware of. Many kittens, on being sent to a new home, may develop diarrhea, a low-grade fever, or cold symptoms. That does not mean the kitten is sick. Actually, it is somewhat routine, usually due to a combination of the stress and trauma of leaving the cattery, the travel, and the immediate adaptation to a new environment, new food, and new owners. To help everyone avoid worries about a new kitten's health, breeders may suggest or even require that the buyer have the kitten seen by a licensed veterinarian soon after getting him home. (Typical language requiring that is in many breeders' contracts, see page 31.)

There are often older purebred cats available for sale. Don't immediately reject the idea of buying a cat, instead of a kitten. There are any number of reasons that purebred adult cats become available. One of the most common is that a breeder may be selling a "retired" Burmese, that is, a male or female that has been shown and/or bred. Most commonly, this cat has been altered, or will be sold only if you agree to alter it when you get him or her home. Such cats can be wonderful companions. They are often the very ones that can get used to a new environment very quickly, and that can make excellent companions, particularly if you are not the kind of person who can take the initial frenzy of kittens in your life. Also, just imagine the thrill of telling your friends that your new Burmese has sired five champions, but you didn't have to deliver any of them!

Your Legal Rights

In a number of states, such as New Jersey and Virginia, specific consumer protection laws cover the sale of kittens. While these laws vary in detail, usually they require the pet store (or in some cases private breeders as well) to give you a written statement describing your rights to return a kitten that is sick. If that is the case in your state, read these notices or contract language very carefully before you sign them and take your new Burmese home (see the contract examples, page 32).

A Burmese kitten enjoying the security of a small basket.

Where to Buy Your Burmese

Once you have decided to purchase a purebred Burmese, you will find you have two major options on where to buy him: You can buy your Burmese from a pet shop that sells purebred kittens or you can go directly to a breeder of Burmese cats.

A responsible breeder has dedicated his or her time to the protection, perfection, and promotion of the breed. Without responsible Burmese breeders, the beautiful Burmese breed would become extinct.

The breeder of your cat probably does not make money selling kittens. As you will see below, it can cost from $150 to $250 to breed and raise a kit-

ten until the age of four months, which is the usual age that responsible breeders release their kittens to new homes. This is for the normal delivery and care of a healthy kitten and does not include any other costs such as stud service or unusual medical care of the queen. It also does not include the cost of the equipment, inspections, or education necessary to breed pure-bred Burmese cats.

Responsible breeders breed cats in order to produce a kitten that surpasses the quality of the parents. However, every litter will produce kittens that the breeder is unable to show because they do not meet the breed's standards as precisely as they should. In addition, breeders are very concerned with maintaining the health of their cattery and can only keep and house a certain number of cats. For these reasons, the breeder will have kittens to sell to selected buyers from time to time. No responsible breeder will ever sell to a pet store. In fact, the cat fancies, cat clubs, and breed societies officially and unofficially discourage, or even bar, their members from selling to pet stores. Given that attitude, you should wonder just who is supplying registered cats to the pet stores.

We feel that there are some real advantages in dealing directly with responsible Burmese breeders:
1. You are getting the cat from the source. If you ever have a question, you can directly ask the person who was responsible for breeding, raising, feeding, and caring for that kitten.
2. You can see pictures of each parent, or even see the parents themselves. That means you can have a good idea of what the Burmese kitten will look like and how big he will be when he is grown.
3. Some breeders will allow you to visit the cattery, so you can see your kitten's prior home. Now, if you cannot

do this, don't worry. Some catteries are closed, and no outsiders are allowed in, in order to protect the kittens from exposure to disease.
4. The breeders know their breed. And they know it well.

What Is a "Responsible Breeder"?

In this book, we use the term "responsible breeder" to separate what we believe to be good breeders from all others. By responsible breeders, we mean the following:
• The breeder's kittens are the result of a planned program of breeding, which serves to perfect and protect the breed.
• If the breeder's cattery is not closed, you should be able to see the queen and sire, assuming the sire is in the cattery, if you ask to do so.
• The breeder will be able to tell you exactly how your kitten was raised.
• The breeder can help you with any questions you may have about the breed, pedigrees, or genetics, or the Fancy and cat shows.
• The breeder can tell you exactly why this kitten is pet-quality and why another is show-quality.
• The breeder sells kittens by contract, and that contract specifies that the kitten must be altered unless it is specifically being sold for show and breeding.
• The breeder is one of your best resources when it comes to cat care in general and, specifically, care of your Burmese cat.
• The breeder will be able to help you register your Burmese kitten with the various cat registries.

Finding a Responsible Breeder

The best place to find responsible Burmese breeders is to start with cat shows. They are held almost every weekend of the year all over the world. This is not only where breeders

A sable Burmese female.

come to have their cats judged against the standards for the breed, but also where breeders join with other breeders to discuss the breeds, cat care, and the Fancy. Most cat shows are open to the public and you can come in to watch the show, see the cats, and have access to the breeders.

Part of the work of breeders is acting as a resource to the public. While cat shows are busy and the breeder may have to excuse himself or herself in order to take the cat to a ring to be judged, the breeders at the show will be more than happy to spend time with you and answer your questions—as time permits.

At many cat shows, the breeders will bring kittens with them that are for sale. If you don't find the exact kitten you want at the show, other breeders there will have pictures of any young kittens that will be for sale when they are of the proper age to be released to their new homes. If they do not have kittens right now, or do not expect to have them in the near future, they may keep a waiting list on which you can put your name for the kitten of your dreams.

In addition to visiting the cat shows in your area to find breeders, you can also find many breeders through advertisements in the various cat national magazines. Most of these publications, such as *Cat Fancy, Cats,* or *I Love Cats Magazine*, are found at most large magazine counters or in some libraries. Copies of the most recent issues of one or more of these magazines may also be available at the cat shows themselves (see Useful Addresses and Literature, page 100). Keep in mind that just because a breeder advertises in a particular issue of a magazine does not guarantee that the breeder has kittens available at that exact moment. Most breeders advertise in every issue, whether or not they currently have kittens available.

Breeders who are advertising in the magazine will be glad to let you know whether or not they currently have kittens for sale. If not, they can tell you when those kittens that are too young to be released will be available to go to a new home. In addition, breeders who may not have Burmese kittens available when you call can often refer you to other breeders of Burmese who do have kittens available at that time. Feel free to ask them.

Another way to find a breeder of Burmese is to access the various on-line services such as America Online through your home computer. There, you can read announcements about available kittens or just leave a note expressing your interest on the bulletin boards that are specifically set up for this. Many breeders access these on-line services on a routine basis and will respond directly to your message or refer you to breeders who currently have kittens available.

When searching for a Burmese breeder, you should also remember that referrals come from many sources. You can ask your veterinarian to recommend a breeder who may be one of his or her clients. Do not hesitate to ask any breeders you may know for a referral to a Burmese breeder, even if their breed is other than the Burmese. Since active breeders routinely exhibit at cat shows, we know breeders of various breeds, not just our own, and we will gladly refer you to these breeders.

You can contact a breeder in person, by letter, or by telephone. Most breeders will spend plenty of time with you and answer all your questions. Breeders generally have a package of materials they can send to you along with photographs of some of the cats in their cattery. Just remember that a breeder's weekend may well be taken up with a cat show that may entail travel on Friday and/or Monday. If you want a breeder to have time to talk to you, it is best to call during the week, usually in the evenings.

When you first contact a breeder, you may well find that you are being interviewed more than you are interviewing. Often you will be asked many questions about the way you live, your knowledge of cats in general, and your understanding of the breed you are interested in specifically. You may be asked for references from your veterinarian and you will most certainly be asked to sign a contract if you are going to buy a kitten or cat.

While the breeder interviews you, you should also be interviewing the breeder. You are entitled to know exactly how the kitten was raised because this information is very valuable to you. The most important thing you should find out is how the kitten was treated during its early life. Professional breeders follow the veterinary literature and know that the ages between two to seven weeks are critical in the future life and adjustment of a kitten. If a kitten is not handled during this period, it may not be able to become fully socialized in the future. Be certain to ask the breeder about this.

In addition, you will want to ask what kind of food the kitten is used to eating and what kind of litter is used in the cattery. This will enable you to make the adjustment from the cattery to your home an easy one for your kitten.

When the breeder says you must sign a contract, make sure you get a copy of it in advance and read it. Ask questions if there is something you do not understand. And feel free to ask for changes if they are needed to clarify what you both have agreed to.

Of course, the best way to find out about the breeder and the cattery is to visit it and see both the cats and the breeder in the cattery environment. Most buyers see this as a great way to check on cleanliness. Also, you as a buyer can actually see cats of different ages in action so you can learn even more about their personalities. However, a cattery visit is not always possible because some breeders do not permit visitors at specific times (or at all). That is what the breeder means when he or she says the cattery is closed. Catteries are closed for a wide variety of reasons. For example, remember that if you already own cats, you are bringing your cat's germs into the cattery. If your cat has a cold, you may pass that cold onto the cattery's cats. When a breeder has a pregnant queen, or kittens that are still too young to have been vaccinated, introducing these new germs into the cattery can be a real health concern. So don't rule out a cattery because it may be closed. There are alternatives to help you to be comfortable with the cattery itself.

An alternative to a cattery visit would be to ask the breeder if their cattery is inspected and certified as, for example, an AACE Four Star Cattery of Excellence or a CFA-Approved Cattery of Excellence. These are special programs that are available to professional breeders. To qualify for such designations, a cattery must first be inspected (annually) by a veterinarian. The veterinarian must grade the cattery according to written standards set up by the sanctioning association—the American Association of Cat Enthusiasts (AACE) or the Cat Fanciers' Association (CFA). These standards cover matters such as the amount of space available, how food is stored, cleanliness, etc.

Remember, passing the inspection means meeting or exceeding these physical standards, but that does not automatically guarantee the health of any individual kitten in the cattery. However, if the cattery currently has such a certification, it does tell you that this cattery meets specific standards for cattery cleanliness and for the proper physical care and treatment of the cats living in that cattery. And, if it does not have one, you should ask why not.

Pet Quality versus Show Quality

In the Fancy, purebred cats are classified into several categories that are shorthand ways to refer to their potential or quality, first as show cats and then as breeding cats. The quality of the individual kitten is based solely on the cattery's evaluation of the kitten. Even though these terms do not have precise meanings, most breeders tend to use the same terms in the same way. The most commonly used categories and their commonly accepted meanings are as follows:

Top Show Quality means that the cat is expected to be able to achieve the title of "Grand Champion" (or higher) in a major United States cat federation in a reasonable number of

Won't you come and play with me?

shows. This is not a guarantee that the cat will achieve that title.

Show Quality means that the cat is expected to be able to achieve a title of "Champion" in a major U.S. cat federation in a reasonable number of shows. As with top show, this is not a guarantee that the cat will achieve that title.

Pet Quality means that the kitten, although a purebred Burmese, does not perfectly meet the Standards of Perfection for the breed as established by the Breed Council of the cat federation where the breeder routinely shows his or her cats. Pet-quality cats are not rated that way for health problems. Rather, this is strictly a cosmetic classification.

These classifications are only an expression of the breeder's opinion. If you think about it, you can quickly see why there can be no guarantee of how a particular Burmese kitten will do as an adult in a cat show. There are many factors, such as presentation, nutrition, personality, and, of course, the quality

of the rest of the field competing that can affect a cat's success in show competition after he leaves the cattery.

Why do these different categories of cats exist? Because of the process involved in breeding the best Burmese (or any other breed of cat). When you breed cats, you use the female that best exemplifies the breed and breed her to the male that best exemplifies the breed. And the designations of show or top show-quality help you when you are trying to buy the best quality Burmese for your breeding program. The better the quality of cat you start with, the better your chances are of achieving a significant title for the cat. And the better the cat you have (proven by the titles), the better the chance that you will produce quality kittens (see Breeding Your Burmese, page 78.)

This means that responsible breeders do not use pet-quality cats in their breeding program because these cats may pass physical traits on to their kittens that do not meet the standards of perfection for the breed. It is these pet-quality Burmese kittens that are sold to the public as pets.

In the case of Burmese, the most common reasons for them to become pets are typically the following, none of which affect how lovable and healthy they are:

• The tail has a kink or bend in it. This can be a small lump on the tail bone, a point where the tail actually changes directions, or even a tail that is curved or bent.

• The body has white hairs scattered through it, or has a white spot, usually on the front of the chest. The latter is called a locket, since it looks like the Burmese is wearing jewelry.

• The coat has "barring." That is, you can see something that looks like the coat has an underlying stripe, sometimes looking like a sergeant's stripes (and thus called chevrons).

Other reasons why a breeder may classify a Burmese as pet quality may not be so obvious to a non-breeder. For example, an experienced Burmese breeder may feel that the eye color will not develop into precisely what they desire, or the length or balance of a part of the cat (such as the tail, the ears, the nose, the head, the paws, etc.) will not, as the cat matures, perfectly meet the written standard for the breed.

Males versus Females

You should be thinking about whether you prefer a male Burmese kitten or a female Burmese kitten. The main issues are really size and disposition.

Size: In the Burmese, as in all other breeds, the males will be somewhat larger than the females when they are fully grown. On average, that means the females may weigh from five to eight pounds (2.3–3.6 kg) and the males from six to twelve pounds (2.7–5.4 kg). Since the Burmese is

A sable male.

such a compact cat, that is really not as much difference as it might seem.

Disposition: It may surprise you to hear that many cat owners (both breeders and pet owners) feel that male kittens are a little sweeter than females. In fact, in many Burmese catteries, you will find that the best "mother" to a litter of young kittens is actually an altered male! And, despite what you may have heard, altered males are very easy to care for. The key is to make certain the male is neutered as soon as your veterinarian feels it is safe, and be sure to specifically ask your veterinarian to remove all testicular material. This will prevent any spraying in the future (see page 94). While this should be standard procedure, breeders are aware of too many cases when not all material is removed, often leaving the males with an urge to spray even after they have been altered. It does not hurt to ask about this.

What Should You Expect to Pay?

It is hard to predict what the price for a Burmese kitten will be when you are ready to buy one. But when you are quoted a price, do not react by asking yourself, "Why does that Burmese kitten cost so much?" If you understand what the costs are, you will be able to understand what the prices will be.

Let's look at the costs of getting the kittens from the queen to you. Then, let's look at some of the costs associated with the queen and sire, such as showing and feeding them. Finally, we'll look at some of the costs of a well-managed and well-equipped small cattery.

We'll start with a litter of three healthy kittens (the average size litter for a Burmese) and take this litter from

A kitten can be sexed at an early age. By the time you get a Burmese, there should be no doubt as to its sex. The female is on the left; the male on the right.

birth to sale at four months. Why four months of age? As we have already said, that's the time by which the kittens will have had all of their shots and can travel safely.

• Some breeders routinely take the new mother to the veterinarian just after the delivery, and that visit alone costs approximately $30. That's in addition to any pre-delivery visits, of course.

• For the first three to six weeks, the kittens nurse. Because of that, the mother often is supplemented (i.e., given vitamins, special food, etc.) For that, allow $5 extra.

• If any one of the kittens shows the slightest problem, the breeder will immediately take that kitten to the veterinarian. The cost: the charge for an office visit and for any medication needed.

• When the litter is ready to be weaned, the breeder makes a weaning mixture. This is generally a mixture of baby food, baby rice cereal, and "cat milk", used for about one week. Then, the breeder gradually moves the kittens onto a ground kitten food mixed with the baby food, baby rice cereal, and cat milk. After the kittens are weaned, all the feeding is taken care of by the breeder. These kittens now have to be fed kitten food and kitten chows. The average kitten will eat one-3 ounce (100g) can of kitten food per day plus kitten chows.

• The kittens need their own litter. Many breeders use a special litter, one not clay based, so the kittens do not have problems if they eat it. The breeder changes the litter at least once a day, so a bag of special litter at $4.95 for 20 pounds (9.1kg) lasts no more than one week for the three kittens. After that, regular litter is used at about 1 pound (0.5kg) per day per kitten.

• Most breeders have the kittens seen at least once by the veterinarian, even if the breeder has given the kittens the necessary inoculations. Allow at least $36 for that visit. Of course, there are extra charges for tests, such as for feline leukemia (FeLV), feline infectious peritonitis (FIP), etc., which the breeder or a buyer want. Before a kitten leaves the cattery, a responsible breeder will have the veterinarian examine the kitten and give a health certificate. This costs a minimum of $25 for each kitten. In addition, there are miscellaneous costs, including laundry, sometimes as much as a load a day for bedding, etc. as well as advertising the cattery and the litter of kittens.

Already, we have spent between $175 and $275 per kitten in routine costs. And there is more:

• Before the kittens there was a queen and a sire. Obviously, the cattery is paying for food and litter for them, as well as normal veterinary bills—for their lifetimes. Food and litter alone at $.75 to $1.25 a day, 365 days a year, for 7 to 10 years amounts to $1,900 to $4,500 per cat. Inoculations and other routine veterinary costs add more.

• We have not yet factored in the costs of showing the cats. A cat show can cost anywhere from $50 to $250. While earnings these titles is critical to

selling a show-quality Burmese to other breeders, they are also a part of the cost of having the adult cats that produced that lovely pet-quality cat you have just fallen in love with.

What does all this mean? To you, it means that you should expect to pay $300 or more for a purebred Burmese. If you pay a lot less, you should wonder where the savings were.

Selecting a Healthy Kitten

Kittens are messy little things. They play in their litter and wear their food all over their faces. They can forget to bathe themselves after they defecate because it is much more fun to return to playing with their littermates. But, in spite of the mess, a healthy kitten, like a healthy child, will always appear to be just that—healthy. When looking at a new kitten, therefore, it is important to look first for these key signs of good health:

Ears. The ears of the kitten should be clean on the inside and out. If you

When you are looking at kittens to bring home, watch them as they play. The bright, eager ones may catch your eye. But be careful if a kitten seems somehow disinterested, or keeps itself apart from the others; that kitten may be sickly.

see any dark discharge or what looks like very dark waxy buildup, you may find yourself taking home ear mites along with your new kitten.

Eyes. If the eyes are runny, you may have a kitten with an upper respiratory problem or one with a genetic eye problem. If the eyes are red around the edge, the kitten may have a slight infection or even a slight allergy. (Cats, just like people, can have slight allergies that are easily managed.)

Coat. A kitten should have a coat that looks healthy. Feel the coat. It should feel good to you and you should not see or feel any dry skin or scabs. There should not be a greasy feeling to the coat, which could mean the kitten has not been properly groomed by its mother. If you feel bumps on the skin, they may indicate flea bite dermatitis.

When you acquire your Burmese, he should already be well socialized. No one yet knows exactly when kittens attach themselves to humans. A responsible breeder will handle the kittens every day in order to make certain they adjust to people and learn that people are a nice part of their life. The bond between humans and animals is a very special one, but it is also one that must be cultivated. The world of humans must be as strange to cats as the world of cats appears to be to humans.

Since cattery cats are socialized at an early age, your kitten should have an alert, friendly attitude and allow himself to be held. However, each kitten is individual and some are more outgoing than others. Don't neglect that little kitten in the corner just because he is not as demonstrative as his littermate. Also, the attitude of kittens varies with their age. All kittens go through a stage where toys are much more fun than people. It seems that they start to develop their loving ways at about 3½ months of age. If

you see a kitten who is a little younger than that, check the kitten's attitude by playing with it using a toy.

So, in addition to assuring yourself that your new Burmese kitten is healthy, try to get a sense of how sociable the kitten is. Kittens are naturally curious. Use that fact to your advantage. Watch the kitten play and watch how he responds to you:
• Does he look at you when you look at him?
• When you offer a toy, does he try to see what it is and how it works?
• When you pick up the kitten, does he shy away from you or does he respond affirmatively? While your heart may go out to the little bundle of fur that hides in the corner of the cage, will you be comfortable and willing to live with a shy and retiring cat?

Making sure you are comfortable with the kitten's personality it important. The kitten you select must be the kitten you expect. You are not likely to change his personality significantly once you get him home. If the kittens you are looking at are not socialized the way you would like, go to another breeder.

What Will the Breeder Ask You?

The most difficult thing in running a cattery is having to part with the precious kittens the breeders have helped to create. As we have already told you, a responsible cat breeder will expect the new owners of a Burmese kitten to meet certain standards. And to do that, they will want to know all about you. It is important for breeders to feel that you, as the new owner, will love and care for your new kitten as much as they would. To this end, your breeder may question you about many things that will help to establish that you are, in fact, the right person to own one of the breeder's wonderful Burmese babies.

Usually, your Burmese breeder will first want to find out whether or not you

This lucky Burmese has a real tree for climbing and scratching.

own a cat now or if you ever did. What he or she is really trying to find out is whether or not you are aware of the responsibilities involved in being the owner of a Burmese cat. If you do own a cat, your breeder will want to know specifically how you take care of it. For example, is your cat spayed/neutered? If not, why not? Unless you are buying a Burmese for a show/breeding program, your new kitten will have to be.

You will be asked: "Do you ever let your cat out of doors?" There are very few breeders who will sell to a household that lets the cat run outside—even for a short time. In addition to creating the risk that your kitten could be bred before it is spayed or neutered, it can run away. Most of all, your breeder will probably remind you that the major cause of death for cats who spend any time outside is the automobile (getting hit by a car or drinking antifreeze).

The breeder may also ask what you feed your cat. Some breeders may ask you for a letter of recommendation from your veterinarian. Others will ask for your veterinarian's name and telephone number and then contact him.

If you had a cat that recently died, your breeder will ask you the cause of death. The breeder does not mean to intrude on your sorrow. He or she wants to know in order to be reassured that the Burmese kitten he or she bred is going into a household where any disease has been eliminated by the time the new kitten arrives. If your cat has died of a contagious disease such as feline leukemia, a breeder will know how to help you to sanitize your house and how long you should wait before you introduce any new kitten into the environment.

None of these questions are meant to imply that you are an irresponsible cat owner. These questions are asked to help reassure the breeder of your Burmese that you know what it means to take care of a cat. To put it another way, responsible breeders will try to make certain that you understand that you will be taking care of your kitten for the rest of his life.

Legal Papers

More and more, when you buy a cat, there will be some legal papers, or even a full-blown contract, involved. This happens for a variety of reasons:

1. State law may require that you, as a buyer from a pet store, sign a written statement explaining your rights if you were sold a sick kitten. In it, you acknowledge that you understand these rights.

2. Codes of conduct adopted by some cat registries and breed clubs require that all pedigree kittens be sold only with a written contract.

3. Even if they are not required to use a written contract, many breeders find that telling the new owner what they need to know and what they have to do is best done in writing.

Just as the reasons for them vary, what you will have to sign will vary.

State Law

Several states (among them New Jersey, New York, and Florida) have so-called "lemon laws" covering the sale of pets by pets stores (and in some cases private breeders as well). These laws are called lemon laws after the laws covering the sale of new cars that are actually "lemons," where the owner is entitled to a full refund or a comparable replacement car. To find out if your state has one of these laws, you can call the state's consumer protection office. Usually it is that office (or the state department of agriculture) that enforces such laws and tells sellers what kinds of forms they must use.

If the state from which you are getting your Burmese kitten does have such a law, that law will require that the seller give you, the kitten buyer, a right to a new kitten or to repayment of some costs, if you bought a sick kitten from the seller. These laws do not give you an unlimited right to return a sick kitten on your terms or to have the pet store pay all veterinarian bills you face with a sick kitten. Rather, they are designed to let you know, in advance, what you must do to make a claim if you think you were sold a sick kitten, and what you can get (as well as what you cannot get).

Following is a composite statement based on how these laws protect you. In some states, you may actually be required to sign a document outlining all of this *before* you leave with the kitten.

If, within 14 days following the sale and delivery of the kitten to the buyer, a licensed veterinarian certifies, in writing, that the kitten is unfit for purchase due to a non-congenital cause or condition, or within six months certifies, in writing, that the kitten is unfit for purchase due to a congenital or hereditary condition or cause, the buyer may do one of the following:

1. Return the kitten and receive a full refund of the total purchase price.

2. Keep the kitten, and receive reimbursement for reasonable veterinary fees associated with the cause or condition incurred prior to the receipt of the veterinary certification. The store's liability under this option will not exceed 75 percent of the purchase price.

3. The right to return the kitten and to receive in exchange a kitten of comparable quality, selected by the store. The selection of the relevant option is up to the owner.

"Unfit for purchase" means any disease, deformity, injury, physical condition, illness, or defect that is congenital or heredity and that severely affects the health of the kitten, or that was manifest, capable of diagnosis, or likely to have been contracted on or before the sale and delivery of the kitten to the buyer.

Any veterinary certificate of unfitness must contain all of the following:

1. The name of the owner of the kitten.

2. The date(s) of all examinations of the kitten.

3. The breed, color, sex, and age of the kitten.

4. A clear statement of the veterinarian's findings and/or diagnosis, including the clinical bases for them, and copies of all relevant reports and tests.

5. A specific statement that the veterinarian certifies that the kitten is "unfit for purchase," as defined above.

6. An itemized statement of all veterinary fees incurred as of the date of the certification.

7. The estimate of the cost to cure the kitten, if the kitten is curable.

8. If the kitten has died, a statement, setting forth the probable cause of death, and the clinical bases for that conclusion.

These laws give you only the rights included in such a statement. That means, for example, if state law limits your medical bills to 75 percent of the purchase price, you cannot expect to have the pet store pay you $1,000 in medical bills for a kitten for which you paid $200.

Breeder Contracts

Some breeders have their own contract. They may have had them drafted for their catteries by contract lawyers, or just adapted them on their own from forms that are printed in many cattery management books. A few breeders are actually required to use forms developed by their breed associations when they sell a cat. Therefore, if you are dealing with a breeder, it is more and more likely that you will be seeing a contract, but the contents of these contracts are not standard; they can vary widely.

The following are sample clauses showing the wide range of issues covered in these contracts. While very few contracts contain all of these clauses, they are all in use somewhere.

Deposits: Some catteries require a deposit from you to hold a specific kitten in your name. If so, the contract will tell you when the balance is due ("before delivery of the kitten") and tell you what happens to the deposit if you cancel the purchase ("If the buyer cancels the purchase, the cattery will refund 50 percent of the deposit within 10 days.") In other words, when you give a deposit to hold a kitten, the breeder no longer can advertise this kitten for sale, so, if you change your mind about the purchase of the kitten, the breeder may have to re-advertise.

Statement of responsibilities: Here, the breeder, using language that is actually enforceable, reminds potential buyers about their responsibilities as a cat owner. That language may include the following:

This award-winning Burmese has earned his plush cushion.

"The buyer will keep the kitten as long as it lives, unless extreme circumstances intervene. The buyer will make provision for care of the kitten if the buyer should die or otherwise become unable to care for it. Such provision does not include euthanasia of the kitten.

"The kitten will be kept inside at all times.

"The kitten will be provided with adequate food, water, and access to hazard-free areas for play. The kitten will not be caged on a regular basis, except for health or similar reasons.

"The kitten will be provided with regular veterinary care, and will have all inoculations kept in effect."

Limits on buyer: Because breeders are concerned about kittens, even after the sale, they sometimes include a warning about reselling a kitten,

such as:

"The buyer is not buying the kitten with the intention of reselling it and any attempt whatsoever to try to resell, lease, add additional person/persons as owners, or otherwise transfer the kitten is a contract violation. The buyer agrees that the kitten will not be used in any way in any clinical, breeding, or medical experiments whatsoever."

This is enforced by a clause such as:

"Any violation of this contract will cause the cattery to immediately repossess the kitten."

Health: You should look closely at all language dealing with health issues. For example, know who is certifying that your kitten is in good health: the veterinarian ("The kitten was last seen by Ima Vet, V.M.D., 2614 Cat Road, Feline, PA 18000 215/555-0000 on _____, 199___ and was confirmed as being in good health. A certificate from the veterinarian accompanies the kitten.") or by the breeder ("The breeder certifies that the kitten is, as of this date, free, of worms, fleas, ear mites, and of any other internal or external parasites. The kitten is guaranteed to be from a FeLV (feline leukemia) negative cattery."). Also, your contract may require you to have the new kitten examined by a veterinarian as soon as possible after it comes into your home. Even if the contract does not require this, state laws dealing with your rights to a refund on a sick kitten may. In any case, it is a very good practice.

Shipment/release of kitten: Most responsible breeders will never release a kitten under four months of age, because it needs to mature. In some states, such as Pennsylvania, they must also make sure that the kitten has had a rabies shot, and many veterinarians believe that such shots do not "take" until the kittens are at least four months old.

Altering the kitten: Here, what you sign can vary widely. Some breeders say that you "must spay/alter the kitten before the kitten is six months old, or as early as a licensed veterinarian will perform the surgery." Others may have had the kitten altered already.

Providing papers: Since you are buying a Burmese, to be a purebred Burmese, it has to be able to be registered. And that means that you should get the kitten's "papers." Here are some options on statements about papers:

Still happy.

"The cattery will provide the buyer with a five-generation pedigree on the kitten, together with papers necessary to register the kitten in the [name of Association], as a purebred Burmese cat [or as a household pet cat]";

or

"The registration papers and pedigree will be provided to the buyer on receipt by the cattery of all of the following:
    payment in full from the buyer (including reimbursement for shipping);

written proof from a veterinarian that the kitten has been spayed/neutered by a licensed veterinarian or veterinary clinic; and receipt by the cattery of the litter/individual registration papers from the registering association(s)."

Right to return: Here, the breeder may use his or her own language or the kind of language required by pet stores. In either case, what you sign limits what you can do if you have a problem, so read it carefully.

Breeding—options/controls: Many breeders insert very particular limits on when and to what cats a cat sold to you can be bred. Common types of clauses include:

"This kitten is being sold to be used only in a Burmese breeding program. The kitten may not be used for breeding any experimental breeding or outcross, color, or pattern breedings."

or

"The buyer agrees that the first breeding of the kitten is subject to the prior approval of the cattery, and that it will not breed the kitten without such approval and consent."

In addition, do not be surprised to see a statement such as: "the buyer agrees that it will not sell any kittens from any breeding involving the kitten to any pet store or animal broker of any kind."

Of course, if the kitten is sold to become a part of your breeding program, you may want to see language covering your rights to a replacement if the kitten ultimately is not capable of breeding:

"If, for any physiological reason, the kitten is incapable of producing kittens, or if the kitten is determined to have a genetic defect that could prevent it from producing healthy kittens, the kitten will be replaced with a kitten of comparable quality."

Enforcement: You may be somewhat surprised to find language on a breach of contract, such as: "If the buyer fails to meet any of the terms of this agreement, the cattery has the right to re-obtain possession and ownership of the kitten." You should know that such clauses are valid and that breeders have been very aggressive in asserting the right to repossession of kittens that have been abused or where the contract is being violated.

Bringing Your Burmese Home

Cats are indoor pets, so you will have to adapt your home environment to adjust to your Burmese. This is not to imply that Burmese are naturally destructive animals. They are not. But they do enjoy playing so what may not seem like a toy to you may definitely be a toy to them. You must always keep in mind that no matter how "human" we think our cats are, a Burmese is an animal and reacts as such. If you have a big or busy home, you may want to let your Burmese adjust to his new environment gradually. For these reasons, many responsible Burmese breeders will not sell a kitten to be brought into a new home for Christmas. Christmas kittens face not only the usual physical and emotional adaptations that all kittens in a new home face, they also face an environment that may be hyperactive and thus frightening, one where they can be ignored just when they need extra attention, and one that can actually be ultra-hazardous to them. For instance, eating tinsel and ribbon can be fatal to a kitten.

Introducing Your Burmese to His New Family

When you bring your Burmese kitten home, he has probably come to you directly from a cattery or from a pet store. In either case, he has already seen people, but they were not his new people—you are. He has also seen many other cats, but not those in his new home. He is young and may be nervous.

All of this means that everything and everyone is strange and nothing is where he is used to having it. Because of all these new things, introductions will be most successful and less traumatic when they are made slowly.

The first introductions you will want to make are the most basic ones. First, make sure to introduce your new Burmese to the area or areas where the litter boxes are kept. Then, put your Burmese in the litter box so he knows exactly what it is there for.

Next, introduce your Burmese to the area where he will be eating. Recognize that he might be too nervous to eat right away, but you still want him to know where the food is. Gently put him down in front of his food and water dishes.

When he wanders away to explore his new home, he will combine his memory and sense of smell to come back when he wants to. Remember, cats have very exacting senses of smell and they will be able to smell their food area and their litter area very quickly. However, a new kitten may not feel comfortable wandering through a strange environment to find them. That is why you introduce these areas first.

Children and Kittens

If you have small children at home, you must make certain that the children are also aware of how to care for a cat, at least in terms of what not to do. It would be disastrous for you to find out that a small child has let your Burmese out of the house and the cat

Learn to pick up and to hold your Burmese properly. Whichever method you use, make sure that she is well supported and feels secure.

became lost because you did not anticipate this. While this would not have been done purposefully, the result is the same. In addition, let your children know the following:

• They should not try to pick up a kitten or cat by its legs or tail. That can hurt the cat.

• They should not make loud noises around a new kitten, as that can scare him.

• They should not interrupt the kitten or cat when the kitten (or cat) is eating or using the litter box.

Also, your children should approach your new Burmese quietly at first.

While your children may want to play right away, let your cat initiate play at the beginning. This will help to reassure him and avoid frightening him. Teach your children how to pick up your Burmese and how to hold him. If they feel secure with your Burmese, he will feel secure with them. If they are too rough, he may be hurt or even injure your child in self-defense.

Picking Up Your Burmese

To pick up your Burmese, place one hand under his chest, and then put the other under his rump. Lift him up, always making sure that you support his full body. Then, you can let your Burmese stay on your arm, or climb onto your shoulder. A brief warning—even though you may know that queens pick up kittens by holding the scruff of the neck in their mouths (called "scruffing"), you should not do this either with a kitten or a cat. The only time you should scruff your Burmese is if you need to control him, as when he is frightened or angry.

Getting More Than One Burmese

Once your Burmese gets adjusted to his new environment, you may run into some typical problems. If you work outside your home, you may find that your Burmese wants to spend his evening with you. Any breed of cat, even the most placid of breeds, will immediately want to spend time with his owner when the owner comes home from a full day out of the house. This is understandable as the Burmese has been alone all day, just resting up so he can play with you all night long! But for you, the new level of undiluted attention can be a little overwhelming at first. If this is a daily situation, you might consider acquiring two Burmese. Many owners do this so that the cats can keep each other company and play with each other during the day. This can help the Burmese spend plenty of quality time with you once you are home, without becoming too pesky.

Introducing Your Burmese to Your Other Cats

If you have other cats, you have to consider how they will receive a stranger into their home. As you can imagine, they may not be pleased, at least at the beginning. There are a few tricks that you can use when introducing your Burmese to your other cats. They each depend on gradually exposing your existing cats to the new Burmese:

First, put him in a separate room when he first arrives (with food and litter, of course). Then let the cats sniff each other under the door. If your Burmese has not been tested for infectious or contagious diseases before he left his cattery, you will want to isolate him from your other cats while waiting for his test results to come back. So this method of separation can be used whether or not you feel it is ideal. As long as your other cats see you going in and out of another room with cat-related equipment and food, they will begin to get used to another cat in their environment. Also, you will come out with a new scent from the Burmese on you (which you cannot smell). After a short time that scent will no longer be new, but rather very familiar.

A slightly different method of separation that also works well is to keep your new Burmese separated from the other cats but still have them see (but not touch) each other. They will get used to each other very easily. You can use a cage or crate for this.

In either case, once your new Burmese is able to come into the presence of the other cats, and they realize that the "new kid" is here to stay, the initial hostility may be over.

Another technique can be used if you are going to put your new

Burmese, like most breeds of cats, love feline playmates. But you do not have to have another Burmese to keep yours company. Burmese are adaptable and will play with any other cat.

It may take your cat a while to accept a new Burmese in the house.

37

HOW-TO:
Cat-proofing Your Home

Even before you bring your new Burmese home, think about cat-proofing your home to make it safer for your new cat.

Cat-proofing means more than just protecting your personal items from being broken or turned into toys, although that is a big part of it. If your Burmese breaks something of yours, such as a vase, or turns your perfume bottle into a toy, he is not only causing you a problem; he is exposing himself to the danger of being cut or poisoned.

Effective cat-proofing means spotting and then removing *all* the dangers to your Burmese that may be present in your home. For example:

Tobacco is a potentially deadly nervous system poison, so leaving cigarettes or even cigarette ashes in an open ashtray is an invitation to a sick cat.

Licking detergent can make your Burmese very ill, so make sure that your dish and laundry detergent containers are kept closed and away from areas where your cat may play.

Chewing on electrical cords that are plugged in can give your cat a shock that can cause cardiac arrest and death, so keep electrical cords away from areas where your Burmese eats, plays, or sleeps. One way to do this is to minimize the use of extension cords. An extension cord that you accidentally move can turn into an attractive "snake" in need of "attacking."

Simple Steps

Fortunately, cat-proofing can be simple and actually requires common sense. Start by thinking like a cat. Standing and looking around for problems is not enough—that is just not the same way your new Burmese is going to approach his new environment. We suggest the following:
• First look near the floor. For example, can your Burmese get under or behind the sofa or the bed? What will he find there? Are there strings to be eaten or open bedsprings to climb in?

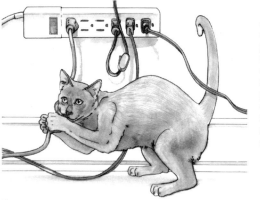

Electrical cords can be a real problem, especially if they are hanging free off the ground. A playful kitten can actually bite through the insulation and be electrocuted.

Cuteness and curiosity go together. So make sure you always check your dishwasher, oven, clothes washer and clothes dryer before you use them.

Where can he hide so that you cannot see (or even hear) him?
• Check for open heat sources that might attract your Burmese. The sight of your cat warming himself by a fireplace might be lovely, but the same heat that brings him near the fireplace might attract him to a place where he can be hurt or trapped. For example, look at space heaters of all types, as well as ovens, clothes dryers, dishwashers, and even drawers under stoves. Make sure that you are aware of these and check before closing any of them. Also, make sure that your Burmese cannot get near heat sources, such as an open fireplace, open flames, or space heater coils, which can burn him.
• Look up a little further. How close are your electrical outlets to the floor (or a counter top)? If you have male Burmese, particularly if they might spray, cover electrical outlets with childproof covers. They prevent harm to spraying cats that use the outlet as a "target," and also prevent damage to the outlet itself.
• Now look up—high. Burmese

38

Common Household Poisons and Toxic Plants

Note: All references are to products that are not specifically labeled as safe for use with cats, such as disinfectants.

Almond pits
Amaryllis
Antifreeze
Apple seeds
Aspirin
Bleach
Boric acid
Carbon monoxide
Cleaning fluid
Deodorants
Deodorizers
Detergents
Diet pills
Dieffenbachia
Disinfectants
Drain cleaners
Furniture polish
Fruit pits (cherry, peach, apricot)
Hair coloring
Laxatives
Lead
Matches
Metal polish
Mothballs
Nail polish and nail polish remover
Paints and paint remover
Philodendron
Potata (green parts, eyes)
Rubbing alcohol
Shoe polish
Sleeping pills
Soap
Suntan lotion
Tobacco
Turpentine
Windshield washer
Wood preservatives

ications, and that can be easily knocked to the floor from table tops or counters. Many things that are safe for us are dangerous to Burmese and other cats. For example, ask yourself, if you are certain that your new Burmese will not be exposed to any common household poisons.

• Look for open containers (such as trash cans), open places (such as cupboards and drawers) and places with tiny (to people) spaces, such as fireplaces, washing machines, clothes dryers, and heavy furniture. Remember that a kitten can get into some very small places.

• Look around, particularly on the floor, and on counters and tables, for objects that can be hazardous to your Burmese if swallowed or mishandled, such as candles and potpourri, plastic bags, needles and pins, threads, yarns, and string, rubber bands, and aluminum foil and plastic wrap.

are great jumpers. What will your Burmese find when he jumps on the bookcase? Does that put him near plants you thought were safely hanging from ceiling hooks? Are these plants safe for cats to eat if they are turned into a salad bar? Do you have delicate items on the bookcase shelves? Even the most graceful cat can knock them over when he lands on a high shelf, particularly if he jumps "blind." If these breakables must stay there and they may be cat accessible, consider using a removable tacky glue to hold them down and keep them safe from accidental blows or from prying paws.

• Look around at eye level and below. What do you keep out that might accidentally be left open, such as cosmetics or med-

Small items, like sewing needles and pins, pushpins, and even thread and yarn are attractive to play with, but are easily swallowed and, if swallowed, they can injure or even kill a cat.

Burmese in with the other cats right away, or if the other two approaches have not completely calmed things down. This depends on the fact that all cats use their sense of smell as one way to recognize each other and to identify their people:

Put a small dab of your (nontoxic) perfume or aftershave both on the existing cats and on your new Burmese. Place it on the forehead, just above the eyes. When the cats smell each other, they will all smell the perfume. Because every cat then smells the same, and also smells

familiar (that is, they have a scent associated with you), they will get confused and think that, since the new cat does not smell foreign, he must belong there, or so we hope.

No matter which method you use, you should expect a couple of days of watching each of your cats trying to exert their dominance. This is perfectly natural and is quite fascinating to observe. Males may well try to mount the new kitten—no matter that they are altered and no matter what the sex (or size) of the new kitten—and bite his neck. Hissing and batting may occur, especially when the interloper dares to eat out of the community food dish. This activity will quickly sort itself out as the existing cats ultimately discover that your new Burmese makes a wonderful playmate.

Interviewing Pet Sitters

If you are considering using a pet sitter for your Burmese if you will be away from home, first, try to find more than one. It is important to try to make time to always interview all of them before deciding on which one you want to use. Ask each of them the following questions:
• What will do they do after they come to your home? At a minimum, they should take care of changing the litter, replacing the water, and cleaning up and refreshing the food. In addition, you may want them to be able to do other things. For example, feel free to ask if they can give medicine to a cat, take time to find and play with a shy kitten, etc. And consider if you want them in once a day, twice a day, or on some other schedule, one that is best for you and your Burmese.
• Are the pet sitters insured and bonded? Most sitters are, and will tell you this even if you do not ask. This coverage is for your protection. After all, you are allowing them to come into your home.

Adult cats also love the security of a basket.

Watching intently.

A pretty platinum female.

• Can they give you any references? If so, you should call some of them. If possible, ask them for references from other cat owners. If you have an older Burmese, focus on those who own cats about the same age as your Burmese. Since the references will generally be good, one question to ask is whether these people have used any other services, and what their experience was with those other services. That way you can compare services.

• Do the cat sitters know where your veterinarian's office is and what his or her hours are? If that office is too far away, or is not open, where will they take your Burmese if there is a medical emergency?

• Do the sitters provide other services? For example, will they bring in your mail, turn lights off and on, water plants, etc.? Don't forget to ask if these services will cost more. While you may think that they are a luxury, remember, doing things like this will make your home look lived in, protecting you from break-ins.

• Will the sitters continue to come in and care for your cat until you call them? Many cat sitters offer a continuous call. That means they will keep coming until you call them, after you have arrived home. This service can be very useful if you are away and weather delays your return by hours (or even days). You will not have to worry about calling the pet sitter. They'll be taking care of your Burmese until you can.

• How much do they charge? Rates vary from service to service, and can even change from weekday to weekend.

Understanding Burmese Cats

Play

Much of what we consider to be normal play is actually your Burmese acting out natural feral (wild) tendencies in an acceptable way. A catnip mouse is not just a catnip mouse to your Burmese. Rather it is also live prey that must be hunted down and killed. So too, a feather tease is not a feather tease. Rather it is a bird that must also be caught. In fact, play fighting among kittens or between housemates is just that—play. While it looks fierce, older kittens and cats have learned to control their play so that they do not hurt themselves or each other.

Watching your Burmese bring his own special jungle into your home can be fascinating. In many ways, the activities of the small domestic house cats are identical to those of the big wild cats. The only difference is that these feral activities have been adapted to fit life as a domesticated animal.

There are many other actions that are not strictly play, but that can be traced back to the wild cat. For example, when your Burmese paws at the floor around his food dish, she is not being silly. Rather, she is finished eating and knows there is still food left. That motion means she is covering her kill (which you call canned food) with the leaves and dirt (or just air) in her forest (your kitchen) to make certain another animal doesn't come and steal it from her. When she pulls her dry chows out of the dish with her paw and then eats it from the floor, there is a reason. It is because she is more satisfied with food she has caught herself than with food she found.

Just as there is a little wild cat in every domestic cat, there is also a little kitten in every adult. If you have never had any cats, there is something else you should watch for and enjoy. When your Burmese is quite contented, she may start opening and closing her front paws, perhaps with her eyes slightly closed. No, she is not

When your Burmese is content, he will let you know by purring and by "dancing" or "making bread." That is what owners often call the kneading motions made with the paws, which are a throwback to when he was nursed by his mother.

Ready for anything.

- The nursing queen also purrs while the kittens are nursing on her. We do not know why. Some believe that the nursing is very pleasing to the queen. Others think it is a way of signaling to the kittens that they should continue feeding.
- Adult Burmese purr when they are contented. Since the origins of purrs are so associated with safety and well-being, that is not surprising.
- What is surprising is that Burmese, like other cats, may also purr when they are ill, when they are in labor, and even when they are dying. Some students of the behavior of domestic cats think this means purring is actually associated with most strongly emotional situations that are not linked to fear or aggression.

Hissing and Spitting

Cats make a hissing sound when they are frightened or angry. The spitting sound is similar, but louder.

Body Language

Cats, like all other animals, communicate in many ways. Your Burmese cat uses the way she stands, moves, looks, and acts as her primary way of communicating with other cats, and also with you. While we may think that our Burmese is talking to us through her purring, her body can tell us much, much more.

Ears. When your Burmese cat pulls back her ears, it shows that she is either experiencing fear or indicating submission. But being submissive is not the same as being docile. A cat showing submission may well be aggressive, and attack to protect herself.

Eyes. Your Burmese's eyes are one of its unique features, showing a wonderful golden color. However, she can also communicate with you through them. Cats, including Burmese, can expand and contract their pupils, in spite of the level of light. That means,

having a seizure (as one startled new cat owner once thought)—she is contented. That motion, which cat owners variously call "dancing" or "making bread" is like the motion she made when she was nursing on her mother when she was still a kitten. By doing this, she is showing you just how happy and safe she feels.

Purring

Purring is one of the most fascinating (and least understood) of all actions. We still do not know exactly how your Burmese cat purrs. But purring means many things to your Burmese:
- Kittens begin purring after they begin nursing, so they associate purring with a feeling of well-being.

even in bright light, you may see contracted pupils. In general, when a Burmese contracts her pupils, this means aggression of some sort. That aggression can be a part of play, or it can mean that your Burmese sees a need to assert real aggression. If the pupils are dilated, your Burmese is experiencing fear. And fear can lead to aggressive behavior.

Whiskers and mouth. Normally, your Burmese's whiskers are extended, showing that she is content. If you see that they are bristling or are pulled back onto the face, she is showing discontent, or even aggression. The same is true with the mouth. If the lips are pulled back or curled, that also shows aggression. But do not confuse this with another important use of the mouth. Your Burmese uses her mouth when she tries to recognize some smells. To do that, she opens her mouth (and usually licks her nose afterwards).

Back and tail. If your Burmese arches her back (actually her spine), she is showing that she is afraid. It is not aggression; actually it is the start of a defensive posture. Watching the tail can also tell you a lot. For example, if the tail is straight up and has a small curl at the tip, that is like a "hello." If it is like an upside down U, your Burmese kitten is being playful. However, if the tail is also covered with bristled fur (or is just directly straight up), your Burmese is showing that she could attack if she feels that she is provoked. The imminence of an attack is often communicated by how fast the cat is moving the tail—the faster the movement, the more aggressive the cat is.

Dealing with a Shy, Frightened, or Aggressive Burmese

Every cat exhibits shyness at some time. Your Burmese may appear shy when you first bring her home

An outdoor cat run may seem to provide safe access to exercise and fresh air, but cats are still exposed to threats ranging from fleas to rabies.

because everything she sees is new to her. Later, when you bring her back from the veterinarian after she has been altered, she may seem to be exhibiting some shyness because she is also experiencing a little discomfort. The females will experience a little more discomfort than the males, since the operation involves cutting through a muscle sheath.

However the Burmese is generally a very active, playful cat who interacts well with humans. If your Burmese tends to be shy, you can either give in

Since your cat cannot talk (well, he can't form words), he communicates with you through body language. Make sure you know the differences among the poses showing curiosity, fear and playfulness.

to this and realize that she will disappear when other people come to your home, or you can work with her to try to help her overcome her shyness.

Overcoming Shyness

To help overcome your Burmese's shyness, you can attempt to socialize her just as she was socialized in the cattery where she was born. To begin with, that means you must handle her every day—no exceptions! Don't be too aggressive. You are trying to help teach her that she can associate affection with human contact. Feel free to reward her with a favorite toy or a treat made for cats.

When someone new comes to your house, let your Burmese have some time to listen and smell. You want to make sure that she realizes that hav-

ing another person in the house is not frightening. Then, carefully bring her out to meet this new person. You may not be able to do this the first time your visitor comes into your home, but try to do it the second time.

When you bring her out for a stranger, at first just hold her and show her off to your visitor. In time, as the cat becomes more used to having other people in the house, ask the visitor to gently pet her or play with her with one of her favorite toys. (Hint: When approaching a shy cat, put your hand down below eye level where she can see it. Do not reach over the head to scratch the ears—she cannot see your hand and could become defensive. Instead, give her a little scratch under the chin, so she continues to keep your hand in view.)

When she permits herself to be petted or plays with a visitor, reward her with one of her favorite treats. Patiently continue this activity and your shy Burmese will eventually come out of her shell.

A Frightened Burmese

Dealing with a frightened Burmese is different. Every cat can become frightened at times. A loud and unexpected noise might scare your Burmese or she may be frightened of thunder and lightning. She may become frightened if a visitor rushes at her or mishandles her. Any of these things are temporary. You should feel comfortable in just letting your Burmese find a hiding place until she calms down. If the fright reflects a cat who is really quite shy, start to work with her once she has calmed down.

If your Burmese has a tendency toward being frightened or aggressive, you might consider leaving a cage or carrier open in a quiet area of your home. She will soon learn that this is her special place and she can retreat there when she wants to feel safe.

The only time you may have to deal with a frightened Burmese while she is still frightened is if she is frightened because she has hurt herself and doesn't know what to do. In this instance, she also may become very aggressive and may try to scratch or bite. The easiest and safest way to handle a frightened or aggressive Burmese in a situation like this is to throw a towel or blanket over her. This temporarily blinds her and she becomes confused. You can use this opportunity to put her immediately in a cage or carrier where she will not be able to hurt himself. She will then be ready if she needs to be taken to the veterinarian for treatment. If that is not the situation, it still gives her a safe place, away from whatever frightened her, where she can calm down. Be careful when doing this. Remember that your Burmese is a strong cat, so make sure that you have a good hold on her and that the cage or carrier you are using is already open and ready to receive her.

If your Burmese is chronically frightened or aggressive, your veterinarian may prescribe a course of treatment with tranquilizers. You must follow this treatment exactly; however, as with all

When meeting a new cat (new to you, that is), it is best if you let her approach you. Extend your hand so she can sniff you. Do not reach over her head, but keep your hand low and in front. If she cannot see what you are doing, she may become apprehensive.

medications, do not try to use human medications on a Burmese yourself. Some medications that are perfectly safe for humans are toxic to cats.

Equipment, Feeding, and Home Care

Basic Equipment

Beds or bedding. There are a wide variety of cat beds you can use or buy. Whether you buy one or make one, keep in mind that your kitten will eventually grow into an adult, so do not get (or make) one that is too small unless you plan to replace it. However, Burmese, like other cats, typically like to sleep curled up in a ball rather than stretched out full length, so a round bed is very comfortable for them.

Regardless of whether you use a commercial cat bed or make one (from a cardboard box, with an opening and a cushioned liner), make sure that the bedding is washable. Avoid bedding that is made of foam, since that has several problems. If the bedding tears, the cat can swallow the bedding and become ill. Some foam products hold odor, so that even when washed, they will still have a smell—even if it is only to your cat. A few foam products can break down over time and develop a smell like urine.

Cat carriers. You should have a carrier, even if you are not planning to go to cats shows with your Burmese. Remember, you'll be going to your veterinarian's office, and you'll need one for that trip. While there are some that are made of wicker or cardboard, we do not recommend them. They are typically not sturdy, and are hard to clean. In addition, the cardboard ones are really temporary cages. In buying a carrier, look for one that is airline-approved, or designed to be used in airlines holds. For you, that means that they are strong, they open and close easily, and are lightweight, easily cleaned, and safe for your kitten. In buying one, do not buy the kitten size unless you plan to buy a larger one later.

Food and water bowls. You can use either metal or ceramic bowls for food and water. Both types can be cleaned in the dishwasher. You might consider getting several sets, so you can put dirty dishes in the dishwasher when you put out new food and freshen the water (which should be at least once a day). Choose dishes that cannot be tipped over easily. And place them in a quiet place, where

A pair of platinum Burmese cats.

48

The brightly colored background shows off this sable Burmese's beautiful coat.

your Burmese will not be disturbed while using them.

Place mats. After selecting a place to feed your Burmese, and setting down his food and water bowls, consider buying a place mat. Putting it under his feeding place will help you protect the floor from spills from the bowls as well as from scratching when your Burmese moves the bowls while he eats.

Litter and litter boxes. You will need a litter box, preferably at least one for each cat you have. The variety of boxes and litter is almost endless. We suggest that you start with the same litter on which your kitten was trained, even getting the same brand, if possible. If you will be using a different brand, add some of the new litter each day so that it becomes familiar to your Burmese.

Whether you use clumping or clay litter, or one of the non-clay brands, you must clean the litter box every day. That means, at a minimum, scooping out any fecal matter and removing any wet litter. Try not to stir up the litter, as that releases the scent. Add fresh litter and smooth it. Wash the litter box at least once a week, twice if you have a whole (unaltered) male or a finicky cat. Do not use any disinfectant not specifically designed for cats. Some, like Lysol, can be toxic; others may repel your cat, so he will not go to the litter box.

Care of the litter box is very important. A dirty litter box is one of the most common reasons for a cat messing, that is, engaging in inappropriate defecation or urination. There are usually reasons for these accidents, such as a dirty litter box, the arrival of a new pet or person to the home, a disruption in schedules (his or yours), and illness. If there is a problem, do not fuss at the cat—he will not associate the scolding with the behavior. Clean it up with a descenter made for this purpose. Then try to keep him away from that spot for a day or two. At the same time, see if you can determine what the problem is. If you cannot see a physical reason immediately, it may be medical. If that is even a possibility, see your veterinarian immediately. Such problems, if left untreated, can quickly become critical.

Scratching posts and trees. These are designed to give your Burmese a place to stretch (so do not get one that is very short) and to keep his claws in condition. When buying one, look for one that is covered with a dense carpet or tightly coiled ropes. They provide real resistance, and help your cat keep his claws in shape. Of course, even the best post is not a substitute for regular nail care (see Nails, page 57).

Collars and leashes. Most cats do not tolerate walking on a leash, and your Burmese is one of those breeds. However, a collar can be very useful if you have a Burmese who might be

To make your new Burmese at home, make sure that you have a good litter box, a bed (or other special place he can sleep), and other aids. Cat toys and cat trees give him valuable exercise. Cat trees also give him a place to sharpen his claws.

able to get outside. The collar should either be elastic or a "break-away," so that the kitten can avoid harm if he catches it on something. If you use a collar, make sure you adjust it properly. Try to slip one finger under it. You should be able to do that without causing your Burmese any discomfort. Put some form of identification on the collar, so that people can contact you if your Burmese should accidentally get out.

Flea collars. Flea collars should not be used as a routine substitute for a regular collar. If they are not needed, you are subjecting your Burmese to unnecessary toxins. If they are needed, you should use them only in connection with a careful regimen of flea control and elimination, conducted as advised by your veterinarian.

Toys. Any store that sells virtually anything for cats will also have cat toys. Some toys are for the cat to play with by himself, like a catnip mouse; others will involve you, like a cat tease. Try both. If you get a catnip toy or even catnip for your kitten and he does not respond by acting silly, do not be surprised. In many cases, the more mature cats are the ones that respond best to catnip. What should you look out for in cat toys?
• Make sure it is not so small that it can be swallowed.
• Examine it. Are there small pieces (eyes, a nose, etc.) that could come off easily in play and be eaten?
• Does it look so fragile that if you step on it, it will break?
• If it is cloth, can you wash it? Remember, the play could end with the toy being dragged into a littler box or into the water dish.

Nutrition
One of the most important ways to make sure that your Burmese maintains his good health and his good looks is to always provide him with the

best in nutritional care. Nutrition is much more than just making sure he does not get too fat or too thin (although that is an important part of it).

Without proper nutrition, your cat's immune system may become impaired. That, in turn, can lead to an increased susceptibility to illnesses. So if your Burmese has too much (or too little) of certain key nutrients, systemic problems can occur. And there is more and more research into what nutrients are important for your Burmese (as well as which ones he should not get). While some nutritional guidelines will remain the same for the life of your Burmese, other aspects of his dietary needs will change, depending upon the age or changes in his health. These changes will be discussed under the appropriate chapters.

When the Burmese was still being developed as a breed, all of today's modern conveniences were far in the future. In addition, not as much was known about cat care and nutrition as we know today. Burmese breeders in the early days of the breed often suggested using a diet for kittens that included evaporated milk, raw ground meat, raw horse meat, and finely chopped raw stew beef. Today, none of these things would be fed to kittens. Modern research has found that cow's milk is not good for many kittens or cats and that raw meat can cause toxoplasmosis.

In general, it is best to start with a feeding schedule that allows you to keep track of what your Burmese eats and how much water he drinks. If you have other cats, that means being able to watch while they eat to see how much each of them are eating.

Overall Feeding Plan
• For kittens and young cats (up to one year in age), plan to feed them 2 to 3 times a day. Feel free to leave out dry food all day in a feeder (called

"free feeding"). Do not let wet food stay out all day. It can become tainted, and even if it does not, it can dry out in a few hours and become unpalatable to your Burmese. So, plan to take away the wet food regularly. That is a good time to change the water too.
• For adults, up to 5 to 6 years in age, plan on a twice-a-day schedule. Some cats will be content with a once-a-day feeding. However, in our experience, having a single feeding of wet food can encourage gobbling. That in turn can lead either to overeating or to the cat tending to throw up some food, neither of which is desirable.
• For older cats, once-a-day feeding with wet food is probably sufficient. If you are concerned about your older cat's weight, you should put out only a set amount of dry food, and stop free feeding.

At first, the best thing is to continue to feed him the same brands of food he was raised on. Over time, you can change to other brands. When you do

Providing a regular, and peaceful place to eat is important. Consider putting a placemat under your cat's food and water bowls to keep the floor clean.

Don't allow your Burmese to turn your living room sofa into a scratching post.

this, do it gradually. Some cats are very reluctant to switch foods, so you can try to accomplish it by starting with the basic food and adding small amounts of the new food each day as they become acclimated to it. Other cats will have the opposite reaction: given a new food, they will gorge themselves on it. Making a gradual transition avoids either extreme.

Feeding Checklists— Do's and Don'ts

Do:

1. Provide your Burmese with a supply of fresh, clean water. Do not put the water near the litter box, since your cat may accidentally scratch dirty litter into clean water and then he will not drink it.

2. Feed a cat food, whether dry, semimoist or canned, which has label stating that it is "complete and balanced nutrition, substantiated by testing performed in accordance with the proce-

dures established by the Association of American Feed Control Officials." This means exactly what it says—it is complete and balanced. Some cat food labels state that the food "meets or exceeds the National Research Council recommendations for a minimum amount of essential nutrients." This means that the diet has not been tested on cats and could mean that the cats eating it are not receiving a complete and balanced diet. This kind of food can be used for a supplement, but should not be used as a cat's entire diet. Other cat food labels will state that "this product is intended for intermittent or supplemental feeding only." This means that the food is never complete or balanced. However, it may be fed *occasionally* as a special treat.

3. Store all cat food properly. Unrefrigerated, opened canned food can develop bacteria. Semisoft food will dry out rapidly after being opened if it isn't kept in a sealed pouch or container. Dry food that is not stored in an airtight container after you have opened the bag or box quickly begins to lose vitamin potency. Also, dry food kept in an open container can attract mice or insects, even in the cleanest home.

4. Feed your Burmese in a quiet, clean area away from too much traffic and also away from the litter box.

5. Feed your cat a diet containing meat. Cats are natural carnivores and, as such, require a meat diet in order to maintain their health. Vegetarian diets are *never* adequate for cats. Among veterinarians studying cat nutrition, it has been said that the best cat food in the world would be field mice!

Don't:

1. Feed your Burmese treats of raw meat. It is a myth that feeding raw meat can produce a Burmese with strong bones or a sturdier body. But, feeding raw meat *could* cause your Burmese to develop a disease called toxoplasmosis (see page 94).

A young platinum Burmese cat.

2. Feed your Burmese *raw* eggs, as they can carry the salmonella bacteria. And salmonella, which is dangerous to you, is even more dangerous to your Burmese cat.

3. Add large amounts of additional vitamins or supplements to a complete and balanced diet. In some cases, this can actually cause an excess of certain nutrients and that excess could harm your Burmese.

4. Feed food that is cold from refrigeration. If you have stored open canned food in the refrigerator, when you take it out to use it, let it warm up to room temperature. If you cannot do that, then warm it (but do not cook it) in the microwave before feeding it. Cold food is not appetizing to your Burmese. In fact, it very hard for a kitten or an older cat to digest chilled food.

5. Overfeed. Veterinarians consider that the number one dietary disease of cats is obesity.

6. Feed cow's milk. Many cats are intolerant of lactose (milk sugar) so that drinking cow's milk can cause them to get diarrhea. There are milk-type products made especially for cats (Whiskas Milk, Alpo Cat Sip), which can be enjoyed by many cats and may be fed as a supplement or treat. But, remember, they are not complete foods.

7. Feed a single fish product as the only diet. Fish are unbalanced in fat-soluble vitamins. That means a diet of human tuna (as opposed to cat food tuna or tuna-flavored cat food) can actually harm your cat.

Special Foods

There three basic types of cat foods, dry, wet, and semi-moist, and numerous varieties of each.

Dry foods:
• are low in cost;
• are easy to store (you do not need to refrigerate them);
• are helpful in reducing tartar build up on teeth;
• may contribute to urinary tract problems over time, if they are the only diet.

Semimoist foods:
• are softer, because they have more moisture than dry foods;
• are easy to store;
• have a shorter life after opening than dry food, since they can dry out;
• are for some cats, more palatable than dry foods;
• are more costly than dry;
• do not control tartar.

Wet (canned) foods:
• are slightly more expensive than dry or semimoist foods;
• are easy to store if not opened;
• are available in more varieties than dry or semimoist foods;
• are a good source of water, since moisture can be up to 75 percent of the volume of the can;
• must be covered and refrigerated after opening;
• are not helpful in controlling tartar.

Cat foods are getting like people foods. Instead of just cat food, we now have an almost bewildering variety of special foods, such as kitten foods, light food, senior foods, and other special diets.

There are several reasons for this variety:

1. Cat food makers follow the same trends that others follow, such as a movement to "light" foods.

2. There are cat foods that are specifically made for cats with health problems, and that are sold only by veterinarians, since they are not balanced, and should be used under supervision. Commercial cat food manufacturers want to track that trend.

3. We learn more about cat nutrition every day.

Let us go over a few of the high points of these different foods:
• Basically, kitten food is designed to provide nutrition appropriate to growing kittens (through one year of age or so) as well as to nursing queens.
• "Light" foods are usually lower in fats, and are sold to help you keep a cat from becoming too fat, or to help him lose weight. Some lower the calories by adding fiber to the mixture. Of course an alternative to help in weight loss is to cut back on the quantity of food you are feeding.
• Senior foods are formulated to be fed to older cats (five years or older). They are usually lower in sodium, and in fats, and may have a higher fiber content.
• Some foods are formulated to help control feline lower urinary tract disease (also called FUS for feline urologic syndrome) by lowering the pH and magnesium levels of the foods. While the commercial foods made this way cannot hurt a cat, it is not certain they help any more than other foods.

Grooming and Preventative Care

Your Burmese cat is an easy cat to keep in good condition. Although all cats shed, the Burmese, with his close-lying short coat, does not shed very much. His fur does not knot or mat and he is basically a naturally healthy breed. However, your Burmese cat, like all other cats, needs regular care to keep him in the very best condition possible.

General

When grooming your Burmese, make yourself comfortable, set up to groom him, and allow enough time. *Proper grooming takes time.* If you have to bathe your Burmese, wear comfortable clothes that you don't mind getting wet. Make sure the grooming area is keep warm and free of drafts. Gather all your equipment at the beginning and keep it easily available. Most cats will not just sit quietly while you get the tooth scraper that you left in the other room.

Eyes: The Burmese, with his big, round eyes, has a tendency to occasionally accumulate dust and even his own fur in his eyes. You can wash out his eyes and keep them clean by using a solution of liquid tears. This is available over the counter in your drugstore. If your Burmese gets allergic attacks that redden his eyes, you can use the allergy eye drops that are also available in drugstores. Be careful when using allergy drops—they can sting your Burmese's eyes just as they can sting yours. If there are persistent eye problems, see your veterinarian for more help.

Ears: All cats develop wax in their ears. There are products available at pet supply stores that, when instilled (poured) in the ear, dissolve the wax and make it easy to remove. You should routinely (once a month or more often) take a washcloth dipped in warm water and clean the inside of the ear of accumulated wax. You can clean the inside ridges of the ear with a cotton swab. Be very careful not to probe too deeply in the ear. If your Burmese shakes his ear continuously or paws at it as if it is painful, or if the ear becomes very red, do not attempt

to treat him on your own. The redness and ear shaking can indicate a problem that must be treated by your veterinarian as soon as possible.

Teeth: If you feed your Burmese a diet that includes dry cat food, the action of the hard food being chewed will actually help to prevent tartar buildup on the teeth. Your veterinarian will check your Burmese's teeth at his annual veterinary visit. Rely on your veterinarian to suggest whether or not tooth cleaning is necessary if you regularly brush and scrape your Burmese' teeth. There are products available in pet supply stores that you can rub on your cat's teeth to help prevent tartar buildup and the resultant gum disease. This is easily done, provided your Burmese is cooperative. One of the best ways to assure cooperation is to build up slowly to regular tooth brushing and scraping. Do a very little at a time, stopping when your Burmese begins to resist. Praise him, and reward him for his cooperation, by a quick play or a small treat. After a while, you can do more and more cleaning.

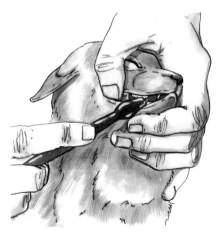

Regular dental care for your Burmese is as important for him as it is for you. And you can help by learning to brush his teeth.

Can't seem to get this basket to stay put.

Tooth Brushing

The Burmese does not have a very big mouth. Use a new, clean eyebrow brush or a small brush specifically made for cleaning between human teeth as a toothbrush. The only toothpaste you should use is one that is made for use only on animals. (As with many other human cosmetics, products made for people are very often harmful to cats—and vice versa.) A variety of these are available at pet stores or at your veterinarian's office. To use them:

• Open your Burmese's mouth, exposing the teeth.

• Using a small amount of toothpaste on the toothbrush, gently brush all the teeth in the mouth that you can reach easily without gagging your Burmese or making him uncomfortable.

• Since cat toothpaste is meant to be left on the teeth, there is no need to wipe off the toothpaste once you have finished.

Scraping the Teeth: Open your Burmese's mouth, exposing the teeth. Using the flat side of a tooth scraper (available in pet supply stores), scrape the canine teeth (the "fangs") in a downward motion from the gum line to the end of the tooth. Do not use too much pressure. If you scrape your cat's teeth regularly, you will not see a large buildup of plaque. Wipe the tooth off with the end of a clean washcloth dipped in warm water.

Continue scraping the other major teeth in the same manner. Usually your cat's mouth is small, as are the teeth, and the only teeth you will be able to scrape are the large ones on the top and the bottom.

Coat

Proper nutrition is the most important step to assuring that your Burmese keeps his glossy coat. Grooming your Burmese's coat is best done using a short rubber brush that

A young platinum female.

56

pulls any loose hairs out of the coat. For a nice gloss on the coat, follow your brushing by smoothing the fur down using a chamois cloth. Unless your Burmese gets into something that makes him very dirty (or has to be prepared for a show), he should not have to be bathed to keep him clean. However, one reason for a regular bath is that regular bathing may be beneficial to you if you are allergic to cats, since the bathing washes away the allergens that cause you to sneeze, wheeze, or itch (see How-to: Bathing Your Burmese, page 58).

Nails

Your Burmese's nails should be clipped weekly for his protection as well as to keep him from inadvertently scratching you. If his nails are too long, he can catch his nails on fabric or on the carpet. When a Burmese is caught on something, his first reaction is to pull away and this can damage a nail.

Cutting your cat's nails is really very easy. The only real trick to it is to get a pair of cat nail scissors that you feel comfortable using. Then hold your Burmese and press the paw to extend the nails. At the base of the nail, you will see a pink area of skin known as the "quick." If you cut this area, you will hurt the cat, so stay away from it. If you cut the nails weekly, you will only have to cut the sharp tips of the claws. If you have a problem handling your Burmese while doing his nails, try keeping all the other feet on a surface. Sometimes a Burmese will feel uncomfortable if he is not allowed to feel his feet firmly on a surface.

A cat tree or clawing bar will help keep your Burmese's nails in shape, but it is not a substitute for regular, weekly manicures. Most difficulties with nail clipping tend to be due to the discomfort of the groomer, and not the

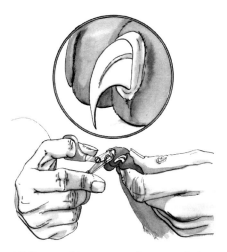

While scratching posts and cat trees help keep a cat's nails in shape, you still need to clip you Burmese cat's nails regularly. Use clippers designed for cats, being careful not to cut into the quick (the blood vessels inside the nail).

cat. If you are nervous, your Burmese will pick up the nervousness and may struggle, causing the entire nail clipping session to become unnecessarily difficult for everyone involved.

Declawing: The authors strongly recommend against declawing your Burmese. There are several reasons for this: the operation involves cutting into the paws, and, if not done properly, can cause gait problems. Removing claws can be uncomfortable, since the Burmese is a very tactile animal. Declawing also prevents your cat from protecting himself if he accidentally happens to get out. Also, cats that are declawed usually cannot be shown in cat shows. If working with your Burmese to use a scratching post and using a squirt gun to stop destructive activity does not work, we suggest trying nail covers, a nonsurgical alternative, before resorting to surgery.

HOW-TO:
Bathing Your Burmese

If your Burmese needs a bath, be certain you use a shampoo that is made for cats (not one made for humans). Cat shampoos have a pH that differs from "people" shampoo. Also, some human shampoos contain ingredients, such as tar, that can be harmful or even toxic to cats.

Most cats get used to bathing fairly easily. As long as you can make this a fun experience, the cat will not be afraid. Talk to your Burmese while you are bathing him and play with him after he is dry. You may also want to reward him with a treat after the completion of a successful bath.

First, brush your Burmese before bathing him. Since cats have a higher body temperature than humans, make certain that the bath water and rinse water is very warm, but not hot. Remember that your Burmese will probably try to fight the bath so be certain to clip his nails first and have all your supplies

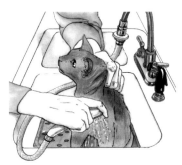

When you are washing and rinsing your Burmese in the sink, do not let the water get too hot and also make sure that you keep your cat under control at all times. A Burmese cat (wet or dry) can leap from the sink in a flash.

around you *before* you begin the bath. Unless your Burmese is used to being bathed because he is being exhibited at cat shows, keep a firm hand on him. It can become very frustrating to have a wet Burmese running all over the house.

If your Burmese gets very frightened during a bath and begins to struggle, grab him firmly by the scruff of the neck (but do not lift him this way). This should stop the struggling. Talk to him calmly and quietly, then attempt to resume the bath. If he tries to leave the sink or tub, you can wash him while he is wearing a nylon figure eight harness. If your Burmese seems uncomfortable in the sink, it may be because he feels insecure, since he has little or no traction on such a smooth surface. You can overcome this anxiety by placing a rubber mat in the sink.

Shampooing
• Using a spray nozzle and very warm water, wet your Burmese thoroughly.

• When your Burmese is thoroughly wet, use the cat shampoo in the dilution recommended on the bottle. Again, only use shampoos made specifically for cats. In particular, in spite of what you may hear, never use any products such as degreasing dish detergents, as these have been known to cause allergic reactions in cats.
• Wash the face carefully, along with the chin and neck, using a washcloth, if you can handle it easily. While most shampoos that are made for cats are tearless, you still don't want to get any soap in the eyes of the cat. If you get soap in your Burmese's eyes, rinse it out immediately with warm water and then follow up with a neutral eyedrop.
• Rinse thoroughly and repeat the shampoo if necessary.

Vinegar Rinses
After you rinse the shampoo out of your Burmese's fur thoroughly with warm water, you might want to follow with a vinegar rinse. This helps to remove any traces of shampoo that may be left in the coat, but it is not an alternative to a complete and thorough job of rinsing. To make a vinegar rinse, add one tablespoon of white vinegar to one quart (.95l) of warm water. Then, pour the mixture on the cat's fur, keeping the solution away from the face. Massage the vinegar rinse into the coat and then rinse the cat again with warm water. If you rinse completely, the smell of the vinegar will not remain on the cat.

Before you start to bathe your Burmese, be completely prepared.

Drying

After you have finished rinsing your Burmese, rub your hand down his fur, getting as much water out of his coat as you can. Then wrap him in a big, absorbent towel, preferably one that has been warmed in the clothes dryer. When he is all bundled up, rub him all over with the towel without removing it. At this point, your Burmese may actually take a nap in your arms.

If you want to make certain your Burmese is thoroughly dry before you let him run around the house, you might consider setting up a drying cage for

If you want, you can set up you own drying cage (metal only) by using a small heater outside of the cage and well out of reach. Make sure that someone is watching at all times.

After rinsing thoroughly, completely wrap your Burmese in a large towel as you take her out of the sink.

him. A drying cage is one where you can confine your Burmese while he dries. Put a small space heater by the cage to provide warmth, so he does not become chilled while he dries. You can also use a space heater that blows warm air. *Never* put the dryer into the cage or place it so close that your Burmese can reach out and touch it. Many space heaters have exposed elements that can burn your cat. Even hot air dryers can get very hot to

the touch, so keep them away from your Burmese. Never leave your Burmese unattended in a drying cage. Remember, you are exposing your cat to extreme heat. When your Burmese is completely dry, remove him from the cage and brush him with a rubber brush. This will help to take any loose fur out of the coat. After you have brushed him, smooth his coat down with a chamois cloth. This shines the fur and makes the Burmese very silky looking.

Health Care

Veterinary Care

Just as humans need doctors, our cats need veterinarians. A good veterinarian is more than someone to see once a year to keep your Burmese's vaccinations current. He or she can teach you various important techniques for taking care of your Burmese and will advise you on home care and preventative medicine, as well as on emergency care.

Your veterinarian is responsible for keeping current on feline medicine and is responsible for advising you when something new is learned about cat care. He or she will help you with advice on nutrition so you can keep your Burmese healthy. If you are considering becoming a breeder, your veterinarian can help you with advice before you assume this major responsibility.

Veterinarians are your single most important resource when it comes to the health of your Burmese. Not only will they share their own knowledge with you, they are also the source of pamphlets and information put out by the various pet food and pet medicine companies on the care of cats and kittens.

The most common preventative care your veterinarian provides is to check your cat every year and administer your cat's routine inoculations. Depending on your veterinarian's professional experience, your personal situation, and the state of feline medicine, he or she will recommend that your Burmese receive vaccinations for some or all of the following:

Rabies. Rabies is a fatal infection of the nervous system that can attack cats, dogs, humans, and many other warm-blooded animals. The virus can be transmitted through the bite of an infected animal. In some states, such as Pennsylvania, all cats and dogs must be vaccinated against rabies.

Feline panleukopenia, sometimes called feline distemper, is a highly contagious disease, marked by depression,

Not all Burmese colors are recognized by all Registries.

stomach pains, vomiting, diarrhea, and dehydration. It can be fatal.

Feline respiratory diseases (rhinotracheitis, calici, chlamydia). These can be highly contagious, and are marked by symptoms such as sneezing, coughing, running eyes, nasal discharges, loss of appetite, and tongue ulcers. If not fatal, recovering cats can continue to carry and even spread infection for long periods.

Feline leukemia (FeLV). This is incurable, highly contagious, and usually fatal. Symptoms include diarrhea, fever, vomiting, and a loss of appetite and weight. The cat's immune system becomes depressed, so that the cat cannot fight off other diseases.

The reader should be aware that there is currently some controversy about the use of killed versus modified live vaccines. While killed viruses are regarded as safer to use on cats, they may not provide the same degree of protection against the targeted illness as a modified live vaccine would. You should discuss the current state of information about this with your veterinarian.

When you visit your veterinarian, he or she will check your Burmese's mouth and teeth to make certain that there is not too much tartar buildup that can lead to gum disease. If necessary, your veterinarian can clean your Burmese's teeth. He will also be able to instruct you in how to provide any special care for your cat's teeth (beyond toothbrushing and scraping) between visits.

Establishing a Relationship with Your Veterinarian

From the very first time you visit your veterinarian, make sure that you understand that you must establish a working relationship to make sure your Burmese gets the best possible care. If this is the first time you have been to this veterinarian, make an appointment in advance and have someone show you around the clinic. This is especially important if you intend to board your Burmese there while you are on vacation. You will want to make certain that the premises and cages are kept clean. Make certain that any boarding facilities are separated from the area housing ill cats and that the cages are large enough to allow room for exercise. In general, all facilities should have proper circulation, good light, and someone on the premises at night in case of an emergency. If you are not happy with the look of the veterinary facility, it is unlikely that you will be happy with the veterinarian.

Establishing a relationship has many aspects. It means making clear to your veterinarian what you know

Begging for table scraps should not be encouraged.

how to do, what you need to be taught to do, and what you expect of him or her. If your veterinarian is not familiar with the Burmese as a breed, it will be up to you to teach him or her about the breed. A good veterinarian continues to learn and will appreciate knowing how your kitten was bred, any special physical problems associated with the breed, and the personality of your kitten.

Once you have established a relationship with the veterinarian, you have an ongoing responsibility to be a good client. That means you must make sure that you ask *every* question you have. Do not leave the office unless you are completely clear as to what is going on, what you must do, what you must avoid, etc. For you to expect your veterinarian to communicate with you, you have to communicate with your veterinarian.

Regular physical examinations of your Burmese by your veterinarian are the key to keeping him healthy.

Your Cat's First Veterinary Examination

When you take your new Burmese to the veterinarian for the first time, be certain to bring along all the papers that were given to you when you acquired him. This will include his record of inoculations (given by both a veterinarian and the breeder) and worming, if he was wormed. They will also show his date of birth and include results of any blood tests that were done on him or on his littermates. (Some breeders routinely run blood tests on one kitten from each litter to assure that their cattery is free from certain communicable diseases. The existence of such a test does not mean the breeder thought one of the kittens was sick; to the contrary, it is done to make sure every litter is as healthy as it can be.)

These documents should include a health record explaining any treatments your Burmese may have received as a kitten as well as the notes on the examination he was given by the breeder's veterinarian before he left the cattery. In some cases, you may also have a separate health certificate signed by a veterinarian summarizing all of this information. If you have any doubt as to what you should show your veterinarian, bring it all. The more information your veterinarian has about your new kitten, the more he or she can help you both.

Also, bring the contract you have with the breeder of your Burmese if the contract mentions anything medical, such as restrictions on the use of vaccines that would void the health guarantee given with the contract, or your rights to return a kitten you think is sick. Your veterinarian must know all of the things you have agreed on that can impact your Burmeses present health, and your care of him. Discuss all of these points with the veterinarian.

Inoculations

Your kitten should have already been inoculated with the routine "baby shots" before he came to you. In most cases, some or even all of these shots were administered by the breeder. The record you are given should designate the type of vaccine that was used on the kitten as well as the date it was given.

There are occasionally veterinarians who want to repeat a breeder's inoculations, particularly if the breeder's inoculation used a killed vaccine and the veterinarian is using a modified live vaccine. In any case, there is no need to repeat inoculation.

Explain any special advice that your breeder may have given you concerning particular inoculations such as the feline leukemia and the feline infectious peritonitis vaccines. For example, if the use of these vaccines voids the health guarantee specified in the breeder's contract with you, you should discuss the use of these vaccines with your veterinarian and with the breeder from whom you bought the kitten.

Blood Tests

Because breeders exhibit their cats at shows, acquire new cats, and may use outside stud service, a responsible breeder will test his or her cattery at regular intervals to assure that diseases are not brought into the cat population. If you have not received a copy of any blood tests that may have been done on your new Burmese, or the cattery blood tests, your veterinarian may want to test your new Burmese for some contagious diseases that affect cats. This is especially true if you already have other cats at home.

Veterinarians can now use blood tests to diagnose several contagious diseases in cats. The diseases that are of most particular concern to you are feline leukemia (FeLV), feline immune deficiency virus (FIV) and feline infectious peritonitus (FIP). (FIV is sometimes called feline AIDS. It is *not* connected with human AIDS, and humans *cannot* get feline AIDS). All three of these diseases are easily passed from one cat to another and are almost inevitably fatal. Of the test for these three diseases, the blood tests for the FeLV and the test for FIV are exact tests. That is, if the test is positive, your Burmese has the disease he was tested for. The blood test for feline infectious peritonitis (FIP), however, is not so exact. In fact, there are now three separate tests. The first blood test shows whether or not your cat has been exposed to the coronavirus. Feline infectious peritonitis is a coronavirus, but there are many others. So, if a so-called FIP (blood titer) test is positive, that does not mean that the cat has FIP. It means that the cat was exposed to a coronavirus,

A well-stocked first aid kit for your Burmese can be invaluable in an emergency. Check it regularly to make sure that all of its contents are still in good shape, and that any medications are still within their pull dates.

Lolling around.

which may or may not have been that of feline infectious peritonitis. Because of the uncertainties in this common test for FIP, no cat should ever be put down because of a positive blood titer test. There are at least two other tests that would have to be run to assure you, as much as is scientifically possible, that the cat may not have FIP. If either of them is negative, the cat is probably fine. (To illustrate how fast veterinary medicine moves, the third test became available during the writing of this book.)

Emergency First Aid

As a responsible Burmese owner, you must always be careful to take good care of your cat. However, emergencies arise. What you can do and what you should keep on hand for emergencies will vary widely depending on a number of factors:
• your Burmese's current state of health;

• how comfortable you are with giving medicine (including shots) to a cat;
• how well educated you are about medicine;
• how far you are from your veterinarian;
• what emergency hours your veterinarian keeps;
• how old (or young) your Burmese is;
• how much help you can count on from other members of your household.

At least, you should do the following:
1. Talk with your veterinarian (frankly) about what you can and will do with your Burmese in terms of medicating it, administering special care, and handling medical emergencies.
2. Pet-proof your home (see How-to: Cat-proofing Your Home, page 38).
3. Ask your veterinarian what supplies you should keep at home and get them. Use the first aid kit checklist on page 65, although your veterinarian

may recommend some additional items.

4. Ask your veterinarian (or someone on the staff) to walk you through a few simple procedures, such as how to give your cat a pill or liquid medicine, how to pick up a frightened Burmese, how to handle a hurt cat, etc. Reading about them in this book (and elsewhere) is useful, but adding even a few moments of practice can give you needed confidence.

5. Invest in a good home cat first aid book. There are many on the market. Look for the following features:

• Can you understand it? That is, is the language clear, are the illustrations simple, and are the charts easy to use?

• How recent is it? Cat medicine changes over time, just as human medicine does.

• Was it written by veterinarians (or is it an edited collection of pieces written by veterinarians)? Many non-veterinarians know a lot about cat care, but it is best to stick to a current book based on the work of experienced veterinarians.

The National Animal Poison Control Center

The National Animal Poison Control Center (NAPCC) is located at the University of Illinois where it runs two hot lines. The first, 800-548-2423 will charge you a fee per case (charged to a major credit card); the second is 900-680-0000, and charges you for the time you are on the line, charged to your telephone bill. If you have to call the NAPCC, be ready to provide the following:

• Your name, address and telephone number.

• The substance(s) your cat has been exposed to, if possible.

• Information about the exposure, such as the amount, how long it has been since your cat was exposed, etc. Also, if other pets were involved.

• Your cat's breed, age, sex, and

A playful sable Burmese.

weight, and any medications it is receiving.

• The problems your cat is experiencing.

Checklist: Basic First Aid Kit for Home Cat Care

1. Rectal thermometer, instant reading if possible.

2. Sealed alcohol swabs.

3. Clean towels.

4. Heating pad (which should be tested each year) with washable cover.

5. Sealed sterile pads of various sizes.

6. Gauze.

7. Adhesive tape, both cloth and paper.

8. Tweezers.

9. Hydrogen peroxide (always check the expiration date).

10. Activated charcoal tablets.

11. Antiseptic ointment.

12. Antihistamine spray.

13. Anti-diarrhea pills or liquid.

14. A feeding syringe.

Care of the Ailing Burmese

Above all, as you live with your Burmese, learn to trust your instincts. When your Burmese does not "look right" to you, it may be because he is not feeling well. While you cannot point to specifics, what you are actually seeing is the accumulation of a large number of small signs: he may not be grooming as much, or eating as well, or acting quite as frisky as he did weeks ago. These changes can be the external signs of illness. Remember, he can't just tell you how poorly he feels; it is up to you and your veterinarian to help figure that out.

While the Burmese is a very healthy breed, all cats do get sick at times. The most common ailments you will run into are those minor illnesses that exhibit symptoms similar to those of the common cold or flu in humans. These symptoms can include sneezing, lethargy, or weeping eyes.

Since you have your Burmese up-to-date on inoculations and have him checked by your veterinarian on an annual basis, signs of a cold in your Burmese should not cause you a great deal of worry. However, just as in humans, a serious cold must be treated in order to prevent it from getting worse or from going into the lungs

One sign of illness is that the third eyelid is partially covering the eye.

and becoming a pneumonia. The most common treatment will include both an antibiotic, to be given only when and as prescribed by your veterinarian, and home treatment by you for the symptoms of the cold. Home care includes making your Burmese comfortable and monitoring his eating and grooming habits.

Another common ailment in cats is an upset stomach. This can show itself in vomiting, either with or without diarrhea. Too often an upset stomach is caused by simple overindulgence. And we are usually the reason for the overindulgence, because we all like to give our cats little treats. We may sometimes fail to realize that too many treats can upset our Burmese's stomach. In addition, Burmese are very curious and active—they may eat things they find around the home that aren't good for them, such as string or plants. This, too, can lead to a stomach problem.

All cats are prone to developing fur balls (hair balls). They will naturally throw them up. If your Burmese throws up, check it for any signs of blood. If there is any, contact your veterinarian at once. It could be an enteritis or your Burmese may have swallowed something.

If your Burmese has diarrhea, before you clean it up, you should look at the stool to determine whether or not there is any blood present in it. If you see blood in the stool, your Burmese may have an enteritis, which is a severe inflammation of the intestinal tract. In this case, veterinary care is important, especially if your Burmese is young. Any cat can quickly become much sicker if it is not properly digesting the food he is eating. And an enteritis may mean that your cat is not able to digest his food. Treatment for enteritis can vary, but many veterinarians like to administer an antibiotic when symptoms of an enteritis are present.

Any symptoms other than cold or slight upset stomach, or any symptoms that continue for longer than 3 or 4 days, can indicate a more serious problem. In such a case, it is critical that your Burmese be seen by the veterinarian. Once the veterinarian has seen your Burmese and prescribed a regimen of treatment, you must follow this treatment exactly and for as long as your veterinarian tells you. The greatest problem that veterinarians have to deal with is the client who feels that the cat is getting better and that the treatment can thus be discontinued. The most common problem is in dealing properly with antibiotics. Antibiotics are prescribed for a specific number of days, and all the antibiotics should be given to your cat even if the cat appears to be completely free of symptoms before you run out of medicine. If you stop too soon, your Burmese can become sick again from the same cause—and this time, your veterinarian may have to prescribe a different medication.

Giving Medications

If your veterinarian prescribes pills, ear drops, or an eye ointment for your Burmese, do not hesitate to ask him or her to show you how to administer these medications if you are not comfortable doing it (see page 70). If you are unable to administer them when they must be given and in the way they have to be used, they cannot help your cat.

Be sure to tell your veterinarian exactly how your Burmese is acting and any problems you have had in the past administering medications. He or she can make suggestions to overcome those problems. If needed, your veterinarian may want to switch medications from, say, a pill to a liquid, if you have problems giving your Burmese pills.

When giving any medication to a Burmese, make sure you have complete

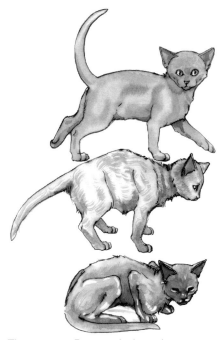

The way your Burmese looks and acts can help you see if it is sick or well. Is it well-groomed and alert (above)? If not, does its fur look poorly groomed and its attitude less alert than usual (middle)? It might be sick. If it is withdrawn and looks like it has not washed its fur for a while (bottom), it may well be ill.

control before you start. The Burmese is a very strong cat for his size, and his strong neck may make it difficult for some owners to hold his head perfectly still when giving pills or liquids.

Dealing with Anorexia (Loss of Appetite)

When your Burmese is feeling sick, one of the first things he may do is stop eating. While this is good when he has diarrhea or vomiting (where the first stage of treatment is to withhold all food), this can be frustrating in other cases when eating is critical to his improvement. If your Burmese is not eating his regular diet, try offering

A mature platinum male.

Common Medications You Can Use for Your Burmese

The following medications, which you may have at home, can be used for your Burmese, *if you cannot reach your veterinarian in an emergency.*

Product	Dosage	Common Use
Vitamin B	½–1 ml.	appetite stimulant
Benadryl (Pediatric)	1 mg/lb. every eight hours	to treat allergic reactions
Dramamine	up to 10 mg every eight hours	to reduce motion sickness
Hydrogen Peroxide 3%	10 ml (by mouth) every 15 minutes	to induce vomiting after ingesting a poison
DiGel Liquid	up to 4 tbs. every eight hours	antacid and anti-gas
Mineral oil	up to 2 tsp. daily	to eliminate constipation
Kaopectate	1 ml/lb. every two hours	to stop diarrhea

him some of the foods he particularly likes. If that does not work, you may try to add small amounts of baby food, either the straight meat diet or the meat and vegetable diets, to his regular cat food to help entice him, or add small pieces of chicken or turkey.

When dealing with anorexia, you may have to go off your cat's regular feeding schedule, which can be difficult for you, if it is based on your own work schedule. You should recognize that your Burmese may not be willing to eat his regular amounts of food on his regular schedule. However, many sick cats are quite willing to eat small amounts of food if it is offered several times during the day.

If your Burmese is being medicated, he may be reluctant to eat at all immediately after the medication. If he fights while being medicated, he may be exhausted from fighting and may literally be too tired to eat. Also, he may have a bad taste in his mouth from the medication, which will make him reluctant to eat. In that case, try waiting for about an hour after medication to offer him some food. While you want to feed him frequently, do not wake him from a nap in order to feed him. Sleep is vital to help him fight his illness and regain his strength and he will probably not eat anyway if he is awakened.

Water
The biggest challenge in any illness is not so much to get your Burmese to eat, but to get him to drink water. While a Burmese can go without food for a relatively long period of time, he cannot go without water. Dehydration can set in quickly in cats and the younger the cat, the more important it is to keep him fully hydrated. A dehydrated cat can quickly loose ground and become more difficult to treat. A severely dehydrated cat can go into shock and die quickly.

Common Medications You Should Never Use for Your Burmese
Aspirin
Pepto Bismol
Tylenol

If your Burmese is not drinking water, try putting drops of water on his paw where he can lick it off. If this doesn't work, put drops of water on his mouth where he can lick it off. If he continues to avoid drinking water, you may have to use a clean medical or

A healthy sable male.

69

HOW-TO:
Hints for Dealing with an Ailing Burmese

1. Provide a warm, quiet and draft-free environment where your Burmese can sleep quietly.
2. Provide frequent, small meals. Use the sick cat or sick kitten diets (see pages 72–73), if desired.
3. If your Burmese is not eating, obtain an appetite stimulant from your veterinarian.
4. If your Burmese has an upper respiratory infection (URI), he may not be able to smell the food and will not be attracted to it. Sprinkle the food with a little garlic powder or tuna juice to stimulate his interest.
5. Warm all the food slightly, even the food that has not been refrigerated. This can make it more attractive by letting the Burmese smell it.
6. Check your cat frequently for dehydration. You can do this by taking a pinch of skin between your fingers, pulling up gently. If the skin springs back to the body, your cat is hydrated, that is, has enough fluid. If it is slow

When caring for a sick cat, provide a quiet area where he can rest but where you can still keep an eye on him.

70

coming back, it may be dehydrated. Offer your cat water often, force-feeding water if necessary. If your Burmese becomes dehydrated, take him to your veterinarian so that he can administer fluids under his skin.
7. Administer medications according to the directions of your veterinarian. Do not stop giving a medicine because you think your Burmese looks healthy again. Many medications, such as antibiotics and steroids, have to be given for the full course for which they are prescribed.

Pills: Some cats are very reluctant to take pills and they will fight against taking them. If your Burmese is amenable, just open his mouth and put the pill in the back of his throat. In order to get him to swallow the pill, blow gently on his nose or massage his throat with his mouth closed. If you do not do this, you may be surprised to see your cat spit out the pill a minute after you have given it to him. If your Burmese tries to bite your finger when you administer a pill, or is too strong for you to handle, you can buy a "pill gun" at a pet supply store. This is a long, plastic, syringe-type piece of equipment. The pill is put in one end, the "gun" is put in your cat's throat (over the hump of the tongue), and the plunger is pushed. The pill is thrust forward so the Burmese cannot spit it out. If your Burmese tries to bite during the pilling, he will bite the plastic gun and not your finger. Most cats cannot avoid getting the pill down their throat when you use a pill gun. If you

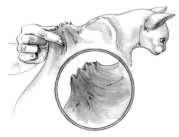

One way to check your Burmese's health is to check for hydration. If you pinch the skin and it does not quickly return to the body, she is dehydrated and needs immediate attention.

have a problem with your Burmese struggling with you to avoid taking a pill (with or without the gun), wrap him carefully in a towel making certain that his legs are securely wrapped and his head is exposed. Make sure you keep an eye on your Burmese for a moment after you have "pilled" him. Even the most experienced owner has been surprised when a Burmese spits out a pill they were sure he had swallowed, even when they used a pill gun.

Liquid medications: If you have to give your cat a liquid medication, use a medical syringe without the needle. First, open your Burmese's mouth. Then, place the syringe into the mouth, and quickly depress the bulb. If this is done quickly, your Burmese will swallow the liquid immediately. If you must, split the doses so that you do not give too much at once. If you try to give too much liquid at once, you may force your cat to throw it back up.

Pastes: Some medications, and many dietary supplements, are available in tubes, in the form of gels or pastes. To give

When giving your Burmese a pill, make certain that you have firm control; then insert the pill over the jaw and to the back of the mouth. A gentle puff on the nose after she closes her mouth will encourage her to swallow the pill.

them to your Burmese, put a small amount on the tip of your finger and then place the medicine on the roof of his mouth. Blowing gently on his nose may help him start to lick it and swallow it. If you are concerned about being bitten, you can use small wooden craft stick, which look like popsicle sticks, to place the paste on the roof of the mouth. You can get these sticks in large bundles at most craft stores. When you use these sticks, throw them away when you are done with one use. Do not re-use them.

Eye drops or ointment:
When you have to give your Burmese eye drops or eye ointment, hold him securely, and wrapped in a towel if necessary. You should then approach him with the medication from over the top of his head. This will let you administer the drops (or ointment) before he sees the dropper or tube coming toward his eye. That way, he may not move his head away. If you come at him directly from the front or side, he will see you coming and move his head away very rapidly. A Burmese can snap his head away from an incoming drop so fast that it will miss his eye, even from a very close distance. After you use the drops or ointment, clean the tip dropper or tube with an alcohol swab. This will kill any bacteria that may have splashed back onto the dropper or tube during the administration of the medication. If you don't do this, you may run the risk of contaminating the dropper or tube with the bacteria you are trying to kill. In some cases, if you do not do this, when you give medication again, you may actually be re-introducing the bacteria you are trying to get rid of.

Ear drops: Hold your Burmese securely or wrap him in a towel with his head exposed. Hold the tall part of the outer ear erect. Place a dropper low in the ear and administer the drops. Then, fold the outer ear over itself and rub *gently* to help the drops stay in the ear. When you are finished, your Burmese will probably shake his head vigorously, spray-

You can give your cat ointment for its eyes if your veterinarian prescribes it. Make sure he is under control so you can place the ointment quickly in the eye inside the lids.

ing a little of the medicine on you, so dress accordingly. Just as with eye drops, clean the dropper with an alcohol swab before you put it away.

8. Check your Burmese's temperature daily. To do this, first lubricate the bulb end of a rectal or an instant reading thermometer with Vaseline or K-Y Jelly. Then, holding your Burmese down with one hand, or wrapping him in a towel if necessary, insert the thermometer into the rectum approximately ½ inch, no more. Hold the thermometer in place for one minute or until the instant reading thermometer signals it is finished measuring the temperature. Remove the thermometer, clean it quickly, and read. The normal temperature of a healthy cat ranges between 100 and 102.5°F (37.8–39°C). Any difference, either higher or lower, means that your Burmese is ill.

9. Do not administer any medications not prescribed by your veterinarian.

Sable mother and kitten.

feeding syringe to push water into the side of his mouth. Be very careful when doing this. Make certain your Burmese is on his belly during this procedure. Forcing water into the mouth of a cat while he is being held on his back can cause him to aspirate water into his lungs. This can ultimately cause pneumonia.

If your Burmese is neither eating nor drinking, you may consider using an unflavored Pedialyte solution instead of water. This product is a water and electrolyte solution that parents give to babies to prevent dehydration. It is safe for cats. If you use this, remember that this product must be used within a limited period of time and must be stored in the refrigerator once it is opened. If it has been refrigerated, be sure to warm the solution before administering it to your Burmese.

Supplementing the Normal Diet

Healthy cats, like healthy people, do not normally need to have their diet supplemented with vitamins. However, a sick Burmese who is not eating a normal diet may well need vitamin supplements. There are many vitamin sup-

Recipe # 1: Sick Kitten Diet
½ jar of chicken baby food
1 raw egg yolk
½ inch Nutracal or Nutri-Stat
1 teaspoon baby rice cereal

Mix all ingredients. Microwave at medium power for 30 seconds or until egg is cooked. Water or "cat milk" may be added to thin the mixture if a feeding syringe is being used. Refrigerate at all times. Serve at warm temperature.

Recipe #2: Sick Cat Diet

turkey wings and backs
parsley
salt
garlic powder

Put the turkey parts in a pot with the salt, parsley, and garlic powder, and cover with water. Bring to a boil and simmer until thick and the meat comes easily off the bones. Remove meat and all bones, etc. from broth. Then remove meat from bones, mince finely, and return the meat only to broth along with seasonings. Refrigerate. This can be served cool in its gelatinous state or reheated and served as soup.

Try feeding a sick cat small amounts several times a day.

plements available for cats. Some vitamins also have added calories that may be desirable if your Burmese is not eating well. Many of these products are in both pill form and in liquid form. Which form is better? That depends on the circumstances. Vitamin pills may be crushed and added to the diet. Liquid vitamins may be added to the diet or given through a feeding syringe.

If your cat is ill, you may want to ask your veterinarian about using a preparation called Nutracal which is available through your veterinarian's office, or Nutri-Stat, which you can buy in a pet supply store. These products contain the complete vitamins needed by cats as well as extra calories. They are thick flavored pastes, and are very

sticky. If your Burmese will not lick them from the tube (which many will), you can easily administer them by placing them on your cat's paw and letting him lick it off. If he is reluctant to do this, you can put it directly into his mouth, along the inside of his jaw.

To Show or Not to Show

Once you have your new Burmese, you may begin to think about showing your cat because:

• you first saw the cat at a cat show, and became interested;

• you purchased a show-quality Burmese, so your contract may actually require you to show that cat;

• you have seen cat shows on television, and they look like they might be fun to be involved with;

• you have read about cat shows in the cat magazines, and, since one is coming to a city near where you live, you are wondering whether or not you should enter;

• when you visit a friend's home who has cats, you admire his rosettes and other awards. He starts telling you about shows and showing, and you find it exciting.

Whatever the reason for your new interest, you should keep a couple of key points in mind before you show your Burmese:

1. If your cat is show-quality, you can show it in the championship class. There it competes with other whole (unaltered) cats of many breeds for titles such as champion and grand champion.

2. If your cat is not show-quality, you still can show it. You usually have two options:

• You can show it in the alter (or premier) class, where you compete for titles like those in the championship class. In the alter class, all of his competitors have been spayed or neutered, and he must be too. In this class, your cat may not be disqualified for a fault, such as a white locket,

which would happen in the championship class. However, that does not mean that the alter class is made up second quality cats. More and more altered cats have previously competed in the championship class, and earned titles there, making this a very competitive class.

• You can show him in the household pet class. Here, you compete for rosettes (and in some associations, titles) against a variety of cats. Some of these cats are purebreds, like yours, which were sold as pet-quality. Some often look like purebreds, but their owners have never had any papers. Others are adopted from shelters and the like, with no information on their history. So it is quite a group.

In any case, before you go to a show, you will have to enter it (you cannot just walk in with your cat). That means obtaining a show flyer from the person listed as a show contact in an ad in one of the cat magazines.

Keep in mind the following points:

• Your cat will probably have to be registered (or recorded) with the association sponsoring the show in order for you to enter the show.

• You will have to get a show flyer and the show entry form well before the date of the show to find out the specifics, such as who is sponsoring it, what you have to do to enter, where it is being held, the show dates, and the amount of the entry fee.

• You'll have to enter the show before the closing date (and get a confirmation of that entry back).

• You'll have to bathe and groom your Burmese before the show (and get him used to being in a show cage and travel carrier).

• You'll have to get to the show.

What do you do when you get to the show?

Carrier. First, make sure you have a carrier to carry your cat to and from the show. Airline-approved carriers are the best. They are sturdy and will keep your Burmese safe while traveling. They are available in pet stores, and also sold by companies advertising in cat magazines. Cardboard carries are not recommend for this type of travel.

Cage curtains. Make sure you have cage curtains that are used to line the inside of your show cage (yes, your cat will be in a cage, probably resting and playing, during the show). The curtains prevent your cat from seeing his neighbors and ensure privacy and a secure place for your Burmese to rest between rings (where he is judged). Cage curtains can be as plain or fancy as you want. There are usually three pieces—one to cover the sides and back, one for the top of the cage, and one covering the floor of the cage. The material should be washable, and easy to fasten to the cage. Plan to cover a cage that is 22″ × 22″ × 22″ (55.9 cm × 55.9 cm × 55.9 cm). Here is one place where even a little advance planning can make the show more fun for you. For example, what color should your cage curtains or coverings be? How about aqua, gold, or brown to show off your Burmese's coat or eye color?

Supplies. You will need more than curtains. Your cage will need a food and water bowl, and a litter pan. While the shows often have litter and even cat food available for your cat, always check first. Also, if your Burmese is finicky about what he eats, you may want to bring your own food.

To keep your cat in top shape during the show, you'll need to have a brush with you. While you'll have to have the claws clipped before the show, you may want to bring your claw clippers with you to trim his nails if they catch on the cage curtains.

Some of the many other things you should bring include:

• paper or plastic bags to dispose of your trash;

• a pen to mark your show catalog (and keep track of those wins);

• a small case (to carry all of this—and the many other things you'll find you need at the shows).

When you get to the show, what then? Well, start by getting to the show early (that is at least one hour before starting time).That gives you a chance to check in with the entry clerk and to get your entry number. There will probably be a benching chart (showing where your cage is, where you are "benched") posted somewhere. Find your number (or name) there, and go to that place. Set up your cage, find the judging rings before they call your cat (by number)

If you show your Burmese, he will be judged after being taken to a separate cage at a "ring"—the judging area.

Curious sable kittens examining every inch of this natural-looking cat tree.

so you know where to go when it is time, and then check your catalog (to make sure all the information about your cat is correct).

Traveling with Your Burmese

When you are traveling to the various cat shows, or taking your cat on any other outing or trip, you should know some tips for safe and easy traveling with your Burmese. Travel with any pet involves careful planning. Keep in mind the following tips:
• Make sure you keep your Burmese from being exposed to heat stress. For example staying in a closed car, even in mild weather, can bring on heat stress in a very few minutes. And, in hot weather, being in a car, even with the windows "cracked" can cause the death of a cat in a matter of minutes.
• If you will be staying at a hotel, motel, etc., call first to make sure that

When you travel with your Burmese, always keep him in a secure cage or carrier. The very smallest, flat carriers are designed for use on airplanes, so your Burmese can be put under the seat in front of you.

your Burmese will be welcome there. Some hotel or motel chains allow pets in all facilities; in others, the decision is made facility by facility.
• Get your Burmese's vaccinations up to date. Get a current health certificate from your veterinarian and take along any important medical records (such as those dealing with medications your Burmese is taking). If you are leaving the state, check with your veterinarian whether or not the state you will be visiting requires a rabies shot. Even if your home state does not, if you bring an unvaccinated Burmese into a state that requires a shot, you are breaking the law.
• Bring your cat's regular food and medication. If you can, bring a supply of bottled water, since cats, like people, sometimes do not adapt easily to local water supplies. If you can, bring his bedding and a favorite toy to play with.
• Even if you do not do so at home, put a collar, (with a current identification and rabies tag) on your Burmese. Also, take along a current photo of your Burmese, in case he is lost.
• Get a large enough cage (or crate) in which your Burmese can travel comfortably. That should give him space to stretch out, to have a water bowl on the side, and a litter box (if he will be confined for more than a few hours). Try to get it well before the trip, so that you can introduce your Burmese to it. Let him go in and out of it, and put a favorite bed in it, so he learns that it will be comfortable.
• If possible, try to train your cat to get used to traveling in the car (this pays dividends when you have to go to the veterinarian). Start with a very short trip (even up and down the driveway). Then gradually increase the length of the trip. If your Burmese

A lovely champagne female.

complains, you can calm him down with soothing talk, but do not let him out of the carrier until you are home. If you want, give him a treat or toy when he comes out of the carrier in the house.
• When driving, do not let your Burmese out, even for a minute. It is safest for him (and for you) if he stays in a comfortable and secure place in the car.
• When you arrive, before you release your Burmese, quickly pet-proof the new area. Remember to find a place for the litter box (and to show it to him). Check for new hazards, such as dressers fastened to the floor behind which he can run, beds on platforms that are open from underneath where he can hide, and toilets without lids into which he can fall. Be creative. One way to protect your Burmese from an open toilet is to separate the cat carrier and put the bottom over the toilet upside down.

Breeding Your Burmese

Should You Breed Your Burmese?

If you bought your Burmese from a breeder with a written contract, and it is not a show-quality cat, you probably have already answered this question. Your contract will probably bar you from breeding the cat and require you to have the cat altered.

Spaying/Neutering

If there is no contract, you should always start with the assumption that you will have the cat spayed (for females) or neutered (for males) unless there is a *very, very good reason to keep the Burmese whole.*

"Spraying" by a male (urinating outside of a litter box at a target) can be triggered by a desire to mark territory or by being near to a female in season. Males altered before they achieve full maturity rarely spray.

The following are *not* valid reasons to keep your Burmese whole.
• *I heard my Burmese will get fat (or lazy) if he is altered.* No! While altering the cat may reduce his overall level of activity, and also affect the levels of some hormones, that is not the same as getting fat (or lazy). If your Burmese becomes fat or lazy, it is probably due to overfeeding or a lack of enough exercise.
• *I want to have another Burmese just like this one.* First, breeding this cat will not do that. Genetics does not work that way. Second, becoming a breeder is a serious decision, and this feeling is not a valid reason to become one.
• *I understand my Burmese's personality will change if he (or she) is altered.* If the personality does change, it is only that he may become a little less aggressive (if he is aggressive now) and he will reduce (or stop) his spraying if it has started. Both are very welcome changes.
• *I think I can sell Burmese kittens and make some money.* No. Virtually every breeder is, at best, in a break-even position. And they have been doing it for a long time. They are breeding to improve the breed, not to make a lot of money.
• *I want my children to witness the "miracle of birth."* First, a pregnant cat will deliver kittens when and where she wants to—and it is not likely she will deliver the kittens when and where your children can see it (even if they are interested). Second, there is a significant responsibility to your cat. You can be risking her health for a lesson. Third, what will you do with the kittens?

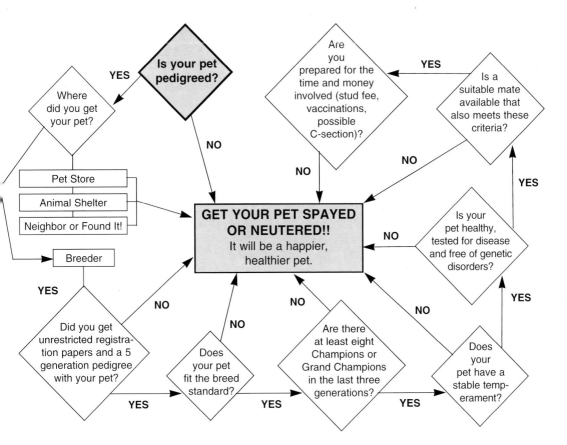

Is your pet pedigreed?

YES → Where did you get your pet?

- Pet Store
- Animal Shelter
- Neighbor or Found It!

→ **GET YOUR PET SPAYED OR NEUTERED!!** It will be a happier, healthier pet.

Breeder

YES ↓

Did you get unrestricted registration papers and a 5 generation pedigree with your pet? — NO → GET YOUR PET SPAYED OR NEUTERED

YES → Does your pet fit the breed standard? — NO → GET YOUR PET SPAYED OR NEUTERED

YES → Are there at least eight Champions or Grand Champions in the last three generations? — NO → GET YOUR PET SPAYED OR NEUTERED

YES → Does your pet have a stable temperament? — NO → GET YOUR PET SPAYED OR NEUTERED

YES → Is your pet healthy, tested for disease and free of genetic disorders? — NO → GET YOUR PET SPAYED OR NEUTERED

YES → Is a suitable mate available that also meets these criteria? — NO → GET YOUR PET SPAYED OR NEUTERED

YES → Are you prepared for the time and money involved (stud fee, vaccinations, possible C-section)? — NO → GET YOUR PET SPAYED OR NEUTERED

Is your pet pedigreed? — NO → GET YOUR PET SPAYED OR NEUTERED

Give them away? To whom? You could be contributing to the miracle of death if unwanted kittens are put down.

- *I am worried about putting my Burmese under anesthesia.* While there is a very slight risk involved, the medical benefits of spaying or neutering far outweigh it. And the earlier you do this, the safer it actually is.

There are a number of very good reasons to have your Burmese cat spayed or neutered:

- Spaying and neutering actually increases your Burmese's chances for a longer and healthier life. For males, you are preventing testicular tumors and probably preventing many prostate problems as well. For a female, if you spay her before she reaches her

When a female is ready to be bred, she goes into "season" or "heat." Even if she does not make any special sounds, she will adopt a characteristic pose, with her tail in the air and hindquarters raised.

Pet Burmese cats should be neutered or spayed.

sexual maturity, you are greatly reducing the chances of her developing breast cancer, as well as eliminating the chances of uterine cancer, ovarian cancer, and uterine infections.

• An altered Burmese is a better pet. Males will tend to be more docile and less aggressive, and your female will no longer attract stray males into the yard near the window where she looks out on the world. If altered early enough, you should avoid having a Burmese that sprays. And your female will not be going into heat, and annoying everyone with the noise.

• You are helping prevent unplanned (and often unhealthy) kittens.

Becoming a Burmese Breeder

In the Fancy, the breeder of purebred cats ranks among the most important people in this very special world. That fact may attract you to consider breeding your Burmese.

The breeder of purebred cats literally helps to keep his or her breed in existence. Without those who dedicate themselves to propagating a breed, the breeds of purebred cats would no longer exist. In fact, some breeds native to other countries, such as the Norwegian Forest Cat (Norway), and the Chartreux (France) exist today only due to the efforts of breeders to keep them from becoming extinct following World War II.

In the case of the Burmese, without the efforts of Dr. Clyde Keeler and Virginia Cobb who felt that Wong Mau would in fact breed true, the Burmese as we know it today might not exist. It took much dedication to preserve the Burmese. Numerous crosses of Wong Mau to sealpoint Siamese cats were necessary to establish this breed. Dr. Keeler and Ms. Cobb's breeding program finally did produce the first true Burmese cats.

Once the Burmese was established and became a purebred cat (that is, when one Burmese was bred to another Burmese, the resulting litter was only Burmese kittens), the work was still not complete. Breeders had to continue breeding the Burmese so that the number of Burmese cats would increase. Many breeders had to become involved in breeding them to widen the genetic pool so that inbreeding did not become necessary. Then, the breeders had to develop the standard for the breed that all show-quality Burmese would have to meet. Finally, the long process of getting this beautiful breed accepted for championship competition had to be undertaken.

What You Need to Know

As you look at your Burmese, you may become tempted to breed your beautiful cat. However, you must realize that managing a breeding cattery is an occupation, and one that can become full-time. You must develop a complete knowledge of genetics, of veterinary care, and of the laws applicable to breeding and selling cats, as well as the laws covering contracts and torts. And all of this education is needed before you acquire any equipment or learn any other techniques.

80

Just as breeding requires much study, it also requires time and dedication. Among those qualities that are required to be a responsible breeder are the following:

1. the ability to continue nursing a sick cat or sit with a queen who is in labor when you have had very little sleep;

2. an understanding veterinarian who enjoys working with breeders and who is available 24 hours a day;

3. strength and stamina for the daily physical labor required to keep the cattery sanitary, clean-smelling, and spotless; and

4. to be blunt, quite a bit of disposable income, as the income in a cattery very rarely matches the expenses incurred.

If you have cleared these first hurdles, there is still more. A responsible breeder must do more than just know basic contract law. The next stage is to get a good contract, understand it, be able to explain it thoroughly and be willing to go to court, if necessary, to make certain the contract is not violated. All breeders hope that those who will provide homes for their kittens understand that they take these contracts very seriously. Some of the contracts provide that breeders can take back the kittens if the contracts are violated. While we hope that this never occurs, these clauses are enforced.

Once having acquired the knowledge to be a responsible breeder, a breeder should also be willing to become a resource to the new owners of their kittens. That is not to say that a breeder considers himself or herself a substitute for a veterinarian. To the contrary! A responsible breeder will be the first to tell you to call your veterinarian if you have a medical problem. But a responsible breeder can be a big help on questions of behavior ("Why does my Burmese do that?"), feeding ("She stopped eating a new food I got her. Why?"), temperament ("My new kitten is fine, but my older

A fine-looking platinum male.

cat is not friendly to her. What do I do?"), medications ("My veterinarian wants to use modified live vaccines. Is that a good idea?"), and related ownership questions ("What other breed gets along well with this one?")

If the new owner decides that he or she wants to exhibit the Burmese, or if he was bought as a show alter, the breeder must be willing to help with that. You may even want to bench with the new owner at the next show to help the new owner out.

Before you undertake the awesome responsibility of breeding your Burmese, first talk to breeders to find out what is involved in managing a successful breeding cattery. In addition to discussions with breeders, look at the books dealing with genetics and cattery management. Also, read articles dealing with the techniques that are involved in breeding. Then ask yourself the following questions:

• Am I willing to keep a whole, working male who may spray separate

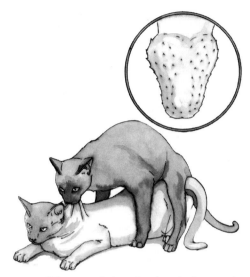

When a male breeds a female, he mounts her as shown. At the end of the mating, the female usually emits a distinctive cry, caused by the barbs on the male's penis. Any whole male (of any breed) can breed any whole female, so it is important to alter your cats as soon as is possible to avoid unplanned kittens.

from the rest of the cattery? Do I have the proper facilities to do that?

• Am I willing to learn techniques such as tube feeding? Am I then willing to tube feed a kitten who may need that kind of help in order to live?

• Am I willing to place or sell the pet quality kittens I will inevitably produce in my litters?

• Am I willing to keep various cats or kittens isolated or otherwise confined in cages when that must be done for the good of the cat? Again, do I have these facilities?

• Do I have the facilities for a separate isolation area for sick cats or for new mothers?

• Am I willing to establish a relationship with a veterinarian who is, in turn, willing to work with breeders of purebred cats?

• Am I willing to clean, disinfect, and deodorize the cattery facilities on a daily basis?

• Am I willing to become involved with the Fancy and show the cats I have purchased as well as those that I have produced in order to test the results of my breeding program against the standards for the Burmese?

Because this is not a book about breeding Burmese, but one about owning Burmese, this chapter cannot possibly give you all of the information you need to become a responsible Burmese breeder. However, the balance of this chapter will give you a brief indication about how a breeding cattery functions and some of the issues involved in running a breeding cattery.

Acquiring the Foundation Queens

Your Burmese queens are the foundation of your breeding cattery and must be selected with great care. Naturally, they must be free of any genetic anomalies and cannot be carriers of any genes that may cause defects in their kittens. They must be strong and healthy and should be as close to the Burmese standard as you can possible get. When looking for a foundation queen, you should make clear to a breeder that you are interested in a show- or at least a breeder-quality Burmese. Make it clear that you will be showing the cat to obtain the highest title the cat can achieve in competition. It is only after this that you will be breeding her. In fact, your contract should include a clause protecting you if the cat cannot breed successfully.

Starting a cattery with one queen and, possibly, one male does not mean you have a breeding program. It only means you have two Burmese who can probably produce kittens. A breeding program is more than having a pair of whole cats. It is actually a carefully planned system of breeding that is aimed at producing the best quality, healthiest kittens possible. A breeding program is meant to extend for many years.

For these reasons, you will want four to five foundation queens who are all as unrelated to each other as is possible. In addition, you will need two males (which you may own or have access to for stud service) who are unrelated to any of your females or to each other. (The genetics behind this policy are complex.)

In terms of quality, you want the cats to be the very best representatives of the breed you can acquire. No cat will be perfect, so you must select queens and sires that will complement each others in terms of producing quality kittens.

A critical concern is that these cats are unrelated. While some advocate linebreeding and even inbreeding (see Glossary, page 97) as a part of a breeding program, such advice ignores the fact that the Burmese breed itself started from a relatively small number of cats. According to one genetics expert, this makes a breed such as the Burmese vulnerable to the problems of inbreeding, even when the specific cats themselves do not appear to be closely related.

Inbreeding Problems

The selection program is aimed at avoiding excessive inbreeding, which has caused entire catteries to collapse upon themselves from what is called "inbreeding depression." Unfortunately, too many novice breeders feel that they should only buy cats from a certain line, usually the line of the Burmese that is currently successful at the cat shows. By doing this, they lose the genetic diversity that is so crucial to the creation and survival of a long-term and successful breeding program.

To find the queens you will need, contact the active Burmese

A mother Burmese washing her kitten is not just cleaning it; she is also stimulating its digestive and elimination systems.

breeders/exhibitors and explain to them exactly what you are looking to do. Do not hesitate to tell them that you are just beginning as a breeder of Burmese. You will need each of the breeders you buy from to be available to you as a resource. Many breeders of purebred cats are very happy to be able to assist a new breeder, so if one breeder is reluctant to sell you a whole female for breeding, you will find another who will be willing to do so.

Meeting with Breeders

As you acquire the queens you desire, bring their pedigrees with you when you meet with other breeders to acquire additional queens. Make certain that you explain to the breeders to whom you are talking that you want the most genetic diversity possible. As you discuss your plans with breeders, ask them if they are aware of any genetic problems that run in various lines. You will want to be guided by what they say, but you will ultimately have to make your own decisions.

A Contract

When you ultimately buy your queen, you may have to sign a contract that

A family of sable Burmese cats.

The reason for this is that a restricted registration usually carries some language like: "This cat may not be used for breeding," "No kittens out of this cat can be registered," or "This cat is not sold for breeding."

In addition, your contract should state that if the queen you have acquired fails to be able to breed and deliver live, healthy kittens, she will be replaced or the amount you paid for her be returned.

Acquiring the Sire

Once you have your queens, you are ready to buy your sires, known as "working (stud) males." Buying a whole male is not going to be as easy as buying your queens. Many breeders are extremely reluctant to sell whole males because the working males will have to live in some type of confinement until they are altered, and, many times, for the rest of their lives.

Some breeders feel that the quality of the kittens in any litter reflect the male more than the female. In other words, they think that the quality of males may be more important than the quality of the females. Since males will produce more offspring than females, there may be some foundation for this belief. Because of this, many breeders seek a higher level of quality in the male. That, in turn means that you will usually find that the male you acquire for your cattery must be exhibited until he achieves a certain title (usually grand champion). He will also generally be more expensive than the queens—as low as a few hundred dollars; or much higher for grand champion. The owner establishes the stud fee according to the value of the stud. As with the queens, it is critical that his paperwork be unrestricted. You also ask for a clause in your contract stating that he will be replaced if he is unable to breed—that is, sire live kittens.

necessitates your having to show your new Burmese queen to the title of champion or grand champion. This is quite common when you are buying cats who are to be kept whole and used for breeding. Since you would want to do this anyway so as to establish the fact that you have show-quality cats as the foundation of your cattery, you should not have a problem with this.

If the breeder specifies that you must show the cat in a specific cat association to achieve that title and you would rather exhibit in a different association, make this clear to the breeder at the very beginning. The breeder may either modify the contract to permit you to exhibit in the association where you want to be or you will have to find another breeder.

Also, make certain that your contract and registration papers are unrestricted, that is they allow you to breed the cat. If you breed a Burmese that has restricted paperwork, none of the kittens in the resulting litters can be registered as purebred Burmese cats.

While you do not have to acquire your working males at the same time you buy your queens, you don't want to wait too long after you acquire the queens. If you allow your queens to go into season too many times without being bred, you may find that you will have problems with them. In fact, you run the risk of your queen developing cystic ovaries or pyometra (infection in the uterus), which may, in many cases, make her unable to be bred or carry a litter to term.

Blood Types

An emerging issue among cat breeders is the research being done on cat blood types. While details on this are well beyond the scope of this book, you should be aware that:
• cats have more than one blood type and their blood can be typed by laboratories;
• cats can receive and give transfusions;
• a breeding between cats with different blood types may produce kittens with "fading kitten syndrome" (see page 93);
• kittens vulnerable to fading can be saved by having the breeder (not the queen) feed the kittens for the first day.

Housing Your Cats

How you house your working cats will depend upon their ages as well as the current situation that exists in your cattery. While your Burmese are still young kittens, they can easily be allowed to run with each other. However, Burmese can develop sexually at a very early age. When this happens, if the cats are not kept apart, you run the risk of an unplanned breeding.

Whole Burmese males, even before they breed, may have a tendency to spray. This is usually the reason they are initially confined. You must make certain that your male has a large cage (usually called a "walk-in," from its overall size) with adequate room to play and shelves on which to sleep. It should be warm and comfortable and easily cleaned. Once a male Burmese has started breeding, his urine takes on a very distinctive odor. It is critical to clean and deodorize your male's cage on a daily basis (or more often) to prevent this odor from becoming overpowering.

If your male's cage is in the same room where you will be for part of the day, you should spend time with him—you don't want to let him lose his socialization. If possible, get him used to wearing a pair of "stud pants." These pants are very much like adult diapers for cats. They fit snugly around the waist and legs and there is an opening for the tail. They are fitted with a thin sanitary napkin. When your Burmese male is wearing stud pants, he may be allowed to run around the house. If he sprays, he will do so in the pants, which are then removed when he is confined for the night. An additional benefit of stud pants is that the cat will not be able to penetrate a female if he is with one you didn't realize was in season.

Mating

Now that you have achieved titles on your Burmese and they are retired from being exhibited, they may be ready to be bred. Your females should have one good heat cycle before they are bred. You will know when this occurs because a female will roll, call, and put her rump in the air while treading the ground with her back feet. She is demonstrating that she is ready to be bred.

This cycle will vary from individual cat to individual cat. In general, your Burmese will go into a heat cycle every six weeks and she will stay in season for five to seven days. When you examine her, you will notice that her vulva is slightly open and she has a clear, slick discharge from this area.

When your queen is in a heat cycle, she can be put in with your male. But before you do that, you should make certain that both the female and the male are in excellent health with all their vaccinations current. They should also, of course, be in top condition.

To avoid having your queen run around being chased by your male, and also because mating must be witnessed in order to know the expected day of delivery of the kittens, cats are usually bred while caged or confined in a small room. If you are using a cage, make certain that nothing, such as the litter box, or food and water dishes, is taking up too much room in the cage. Also, be aware that if your queen appears reluctant to be bred, the male will make several attempts even if she keeps jumping out of his way. If there are too many loose items in the breeding cage, they can end up being scattered all over the place. They may also get in the way and inhibit a successful mating.

Make certain that the cage itself is not too slick. Having a carpeted shelf in a breeding cage is very useful. Cages made of PVC piping and flooring are excellent for housing whole cats, but may be too slippery to use as a breeding cage.

When breeding occurs, the male will grab the queen by the back of the neck and penetrate her. Once ejaculation has occurred, the male will disconnect himself from the female. The penis on a male cat is barbed and when he withdraws it from the female, he causes her some pain. At this point, she will usually cry out and may turn on the male. For this reason, all nails should be clipped prior to breeding. Also, a shelf should be provided where the male can get away from the female. After the mating cry, the female will roll around and wash herself.

When you see (and hear) this happen, mark it on your calendar. This enables you to begin counting days until the delivery is expected to take place. Most breeders feel that a queen should be bred two or three times a day for no more than three days. You will have to decide for yourself how long you feel you should keep your cats together in the breeding cage. If the female appears to be too uncomfortable during breeding or if several breedings occur in rapid succession, you may not want to keep the cats together for too long.

Once the witnessed mating has occurred, you should immediately begin to treat your Burmese as if she is pregnant.

Pregnancy

Your Burmese will be pregnant for anywhere from 63 to 69 days. After your female has had one litter, she will tend to stay on the same schedule for future litters. During this time she will be getting nourishment from her food for both herself and for her growing kittens. For this reason, many breeders will supplement the pregnant queen's diet with extra vitamins or calcium. If you are feeding a completely balanced, nutritionally complete diet, this is not really necessary. You must, however, make certain that your Burmese has adequate amounts of food. She will eat more than she formerly did. This increased appetite will continue throughout her period of lactation.

The first sign of pregnancy that you will notice is called "pinking up," when the queen's nipples become more apparent and begin to turn pink. This can occur as soon as ten days after she was bred, but more often takes up to three weeks. However, some cats don't really pink up so if you don't see this, you should continue to treat your queen as if she is pregnant. You will gradually notice your Burmese becoming rounder. Depending upon how many kittens she is carrying, and how big they are, she may become very large by the time she is due to deliver. Your Burmese queen will begin to curtail her own activity as her pregnancy progresses.

Before your queen is due to deliver, she should be checked by your veterinarian. You may wish to have her X-rayed at the appropriate time, which is in the final stages, usually after 45 days. This will enable you to determine how many kittens she is carrying. If there is a problem, you might consider having your Burmese queen have an ultrasound of her abdomen. When this is done, you can actually see the heartbeats of the kittens and you will know whether or not the kittens appear viable at that time.

Kittening

The week before your queen is due to deliver, you should confine her in the cage where she will deliver her babies and where she will stay while they are maturing into kittens. This cage should be large enough to hold the delivery box in addition to a bed, litter box, food dish, and water bowl.

Since the delivery box must be warm, many breeders buy a special piece of equipment for this purpose— a bed made of plastic, filled with water, and plugged into an electrical socket. It has a thermostat to control the temperature. If you do not want to invest in this, you may use a heating pad, set on low, that is then covered with cloth. (Diapers or soft towels can be used for this purpose.) When using a heating pad, you must be certain that it does not develop hot spots where the queen or the kittens could get burned.

When she goes into labor, your queen should be under your constant observation. Problems (which are well

beyond the scope of this book) do occur during delivery and you must be prepared for a problem just as you must be prepared to deliver the kittens if there is no problem. You should carefully note the time that labor started.

Once the delivery starts, you should also note the time each kitten is delivered, the kitten's weight, sex, color, and any problems that were apparent. If you are breeding a sable Burmese to a sable Burmese, you must find some way to distinguish each kitten. One easy way to do this is to put a drop of iodine on a different place on each kitten as he or she is delivered. For example, your notes might read:

Kitten #1: 2½ ounces (71g): male: sable: iodine on right ear,
Kitten #2: 3 ounces (100g): male: sable: breech birth: iodine on left ear,
Kitten #3: 2½ ounces (71g): female: iodine on right front pad.

Now that your Burmese queen has delivered her kittens, you must care for her as well as the new babies. While the queen will take care of the kittens, feeding them and litter-training them, you will have to check the babies every day. They should be weighed and evaluated so that you can immediately be aware if something is going wrong.

You will have the responsibility of weaning the kittens, socializing them, evaluating their quality, and placing them in excellent homes. You will laugh at them, love them, and cry when they have to leave the cattery. There is joy and sorrow in being a breeder of purebred Burmese cats. But through it all, if you can live this kind of life, you will know that you did something to keep this beautiful breed from becoming extinct.

Care of the Older Burmese

Every year, as new advances are made in feline veterinary medicine, the lifespan of a Burmese increases. In our lifetime alone, we have personally seen the average lifespan of a cat go from 7 years to 15 years and more. But, just as with humans, some adjustments in lifestyle will naturally come about as a part of the aging process.

Over time your Burmese will act and look different. He will slow down with age and may sleep more. He will be less tolerant of the stresses that a young cat adapts to normally. He may become set in his ways and become more irritable if he has to go to the veterinarian or has to be boarded while you go on vacation. This is a normal part of the life of your Burmese.

Even the way he looks may change. His coat may start to look a little thin-

ner. If he is one of the pastel colors, his coat may actually get darker as he gets older, because his circulation (which is slowing down, just like ours) has an indirect impact on his coat color.

By the time you see these changes, the relationship you have developed with your friend of many years will have solidified. He is now your companion, one you can talk to and spend quiet time with. These are special years for both of you. Remember, your Burmese is not the only one who may be experiencing the slowing down that comes with age.

Watching your older Burmese carefully will enable you to adjust his environment to any physical changes that may have occurred within him. For example, if your Burmese has developed arthritis, he may find it easier to

An older Burmese devotes more time to simple relaxation.

have a larger litter box or a step that goes up to it. He may also want an extra towel or blanket if he feels cold when sitting on the floor. The height of his food dish may have to be adjusted to enable him to eat more easily. You will learn what he needs by watching him and anticipating his needs. This is also the time to make certain you keep up with your grooming regimen. Keeping the loose hair out of his coat will help avoid hair balls or constipation. Tooth cleaning is also critical at this time to help prevent gingivitis, which can cause loss of teeth and subsequent difficulties eating.

As your Burmese ages, also talk with your veterinarian about inoculations. Some veterinarians will eliminate specific shots or change the type of vaccine they want to use on an older cat. Your veterinarian can also tell you how to check for signs of incipient illnesses that can affect the older cat. He or she may also want to increase the yearly visits to twice per year.

As your Burmese matures, she will become even closer to you, and will usually spend more time with you each day.

Nutritional Changes

If your Burmese is still enjoying his regular, balanced diet, there is no need to change it. The biggest problem that the older Burmese experiences is a tendency to gain weight as his activity level decreases. If he is naturally eating less, and many cats will adjust their diets themselves, you have nothing to worry about. If your Burmese has gained weight and still eats as much as he did when he was younger, you can buy cat food, both dry and canned, that is formulated especially for senior cats. Such foods, available both from your veterinarian and, increasingly, in grocery stores, reduce sodium and fats, and try to include products that are easier to digest. Most cats make an easy transition to this diet, especially if it is introduced slowly.

Unless your Burmese is on a special diet for a medical problem, supplements are not needed even though he is now older. If you have to feed a special diet for some reason, check with your veterinarian as to the advisability of nutritional supplements. If your Burmese has developed anorexia, he may be prescribed an appetite stimulant to help remedy this condition. While diarrhea and constipation are more common in the older Burmese, they may also be signs of illness. If either of these symptoms persists for more than a couple of days, consult your veterinarian.

Normal Infirmities of Aging

Just as there are common diseases of older humans, there are also common diseases of the older Burmese. Today, most of these diseases can be controlled, if not cured. As long as your Burmese retains a good quality of life, you can work with any illness he might have. Among the most common diseases of the older cat are the following:

Anemia: This is not uncommon in the older cat and is easily treated.

Diabetes mellitus: Diabetes in the Burmese can be controlled through diet and, if necessary, administration of a daily dose of insulin.

Feline lower urinary tract disease: This is an inflammation of the urinary tract, which can result in a complete obstruction of the urethra. If diagnosed early, it can be treated by a combination of antibiotics and dietary management.

Heart disease: The most common problem seen in veterinary practice is congestive heart failure. This is due to the failure of heart valves to close properly and results in the accumulation of fluid in the body.

Hyperthyroidism: This disease of the thyroid gland is easily treated with medication.

Kidney disease or failure: Kidney failure is not uncommon in older cats. Medication and a low protein diet can be used when kidney failure is present.

Liver disease: Like kidney malfunction, this cannot be cured but can be managed through diet.

Your older Burmese needs more help to stay well groomed. His coat may become so thin that you can gently groom him with a comb.

Periodontal disease: Gum and tooth disease may be found in more than half of all cats six years old and older. If diagnosed in the early stages, it is reversible.

Tumors: Just as cancer can affect humans, so can it affect cats. Some tumors can be removed surgically and may not recur. If the cancer has metastasized, radiation and chemotherapy may be successful.

Euthanasia

If your senior Burmese is suffering, your veterinarian will discuss euthanasia with you. Remember that this cat is your friend and has been for many years. While the decision to euthanize is yours—and the decision is a difficult one—keep in mind how your Burmese lived his life and, if you feel that he no longer has a comfortable life, do not regret granting him the peace that euthanasia can bring.

What If You Are Not There?

Realistically, most of us do not plan for the possibility that our cats will still be alive after we have died. And, among those that do make plans, even that is fairly informal.

If you should be injured and hospitalized, does anyone else know you have a Burmese, and do they have the ability to step in immediately? If you are older, or in poor health, you could find that you may be put under a guardianship to help you manage your assets and to help you care for yourself. But that means someone else will be making decisions about your Burmese, not you.

Each of these alternatives appears clear, but remember, they are really just points on a spectrum. For example, if you die, and your Burmese survives you, the issue is not just leaving money to care for the cat in the long run. What happens in the short run? Who feeds your cat today and tomorrow? And for how long, and where?

In any case, you have to be realistic—you have to consider what options you really have, and what ones you are willing to consider.

For example, you may wonder whether you can order that your Burmese be destroyed on your death. Understand that your authors do not believe in this, but it is a question that some people have asked. The answer is probably not. Even though a pet cat is still seen as having no monetary value, the courts that supervise the way estates are run have been reluctant to order pets destroyed by order of their now-deceased owners.

Leaving Money

Can you just leave some money to your Burmese? In one word—no. We have probably heard the same stories you have about someone leaving millions (and it is always millions) to Brownie. Realistically, you just cannot do that. In fact, if you try this, and it is challenged successfully, one of the following may happen:

• The court may convert the bequest (the money you left) into a trust for the benefit of the pet (if that is even legal in your state).

• The court may invalidate the bequest completely, leaving the money to those who will already get the bulk of the estate.

• The court may invalidate the entire will. This means it is letting the money go by "intestacy" (outside of the will), as dictated by state law. Typically, that is to the closest blood relatives.

Can you leave money in trust for your Burmese? For a number of fairly antique reasons, it has always been regarded as virtually impossible to leave money in trust for a single animal (or all of your animals), as opposed to creating a trust to benefit animals as a whole. However, the laws governing trusts in many states have been changing over the years, making these old objections less important, if not removing them completely.

Leaving Your Cat to Someone

Can you just leave your Burmese to someone else? Yes. But just doing that in your will does not automatically solve your problem. A cat is personal property. That means someone can either accept the cat, and care for it, accept the cat, then sell it, destroy it, or just ignore it, or refuse to accept it. It is that person's choice—and you cannot force them to do something they do not want to do. So, don't just leave the cat to someone without talking to them, and being comfortable with them. Make sure they know what is involved, and are willing to accept the cat.

By this point, you are wondering, can I just leave my money and my Burmese to someone? This is probably the most common approach, and also one that makes a lot of sense. The most common effort is to leave money to a named person on the condition that the person care for the cat, or for the person to be left money *and* the cat, with a request that the money be used to care for the cat. While seeming to accomplish what the owner wants, however, such efforts, if challenged, generally are not allowed. Even if they are, this does not end your need to plan.

Here is a bit of cold, hard, legal information. If you leave your Burmese to someone, say John, with money to care for her, that does not guarantee it will happen that way. John can either take the cat and money and care for her, as you intend, take the cat and money, but use the money for his own ends, take the cat and money, and then give away, sell, or destroy the cat, or just take the money and refuse the cat.

All in all, it boils down to answering the question: Who might be willing to take my Burmese? And that can be a tough one to answer. First, start with where you got your Burmese. If you bought a pet from a breeder, check the contract you signed. Some breeders agree to take back cats (for a limited period of time), or to help place a cat if you can no longer keep it. Even if that is not in the contract, or you do not have a written contract, the breeder may be able to help you (or your estate) place the cat.

Next, turn to other sources. Friends, family, and the like, of course should be considered. But be careful, and be realistic. Never assume that because your sister appears to love your Burmese, she will be happy to bring it into her home with her three children and two dogs. Ask her, and then consider her answer very carefully. Other friends who have cats may be willing to take them, but, again check.

In any case, be realistic. If you are 55, do you really think it is a good idea to arrange for your 71-year-old sister to care for your Burmese when you die? Especially if your cat is two years old now. That might eventually mean having a 84-year-old woman caring for a 15-year-old cat. Think about it—from both sides.

Facilities

Another option is to arrange for your Burmese to be placed in a long-term or permanent care, no-kill facility. In the former case, the facility cares for your cat while working to place it in a permanent home. In the latter, the cat stays in the facility permanently. Several issues are involved in the decision to use such facilities:

• First, as with any other option in caring for your cat, planning is vital. Most of these groups of both types require that you contact them first. In addition, you will have to make specific financial arrangements with them;

• Second, you have to consider whether or not your Burmese will be happy living, for a short time or permanently, in such a facility. Some groups, among them the Humane Society, have argued that many of these facilities take in more animals than they can properly care for.

Companion Animal Groups

Another option is to contact groups that use companion animals for a number of purposes. These may agree to take the cat, usually if arrangements are made in advance. But that may be conditioned on their ability to use the cat, the cat's age and condition, and other factors.

Regardless of what option you elect to use in planning for your cat after your death, or in case of your disability, you have to make sure that you have someone who will do what you want. That means you must take the time to find someone (or some group) on whom or on which you can rely to carry out your wishes. But don't stop there. Contact the person or group and make your intentions clear. Make sure that others who know you understand that you have made arrangements for your cats. To be blunt, if the people who come across your cats after your death do not know what you have planned for them, they will do what *they* think is best. Your wishes may never be carried out because your wishes are not known.

Glossary

AACE American Association of Cat Enthusiasts, a cat federation.

ACA American Cat Association, the oldest U.S. cat federation.

ACFA The American Cat Fanciers' Association, Inc., a cat federation.

ADULT For purposes of cat shows, a cat that is at least eight months old. The age is determined at the time of the show.

ALL-BREED RING A ring where longhair cats and shorthair cats are judged against each other.

ALLELES Mutated genes.

ALTER A class where spayed and neutered cats are judged (see *Premier*). Also, a cat that has been surgically corrected to prevent breeding. (See *Neuter* and *Spay*.)

BENCHED CAT A cat that is present and qualified for competition at a cat show.

BEST OF THE BEST An award given at the end of a cat show to the cat, kitten, alter/premier, household pet cat, and household pet kitten that scored highest during the entire show.

BREED CLUB A group of cat owners and exhibitors where membership is limited to owners of the breed in question. It may be independent or affiliated with one of the cat registries.

BREED STANDARDS Those standards formulated by a cat federation for use in judging a particular breed. These standards are the ideal for that breed. They are sometimes called "Standards of Perfection."

CAT FANCY A term used to encompass those breeding purebred cats and showing both purebred and household pet cats at cat shows. There it is usually just called "the Fancy." It is also used to mean a cat federation.

CAT FEDERATION An association of persons and clubs involved in breeding, showing, and judging cats. Among its activities are sanctioning shows and registering cats. (See also *Registry*.)

CAT A feline, of either sex, over eight months of age.

CATALOGUE The official record of all cats entered in a particular show.

CATTERY A name registered by a cat breeder to identify the breeder's line of breeding. A registered cattery name always appears as a prefix to the name of a cat bred by that cattery/breeder.

CFA The Cat Fanciers' Association, Inc., a cat federation.

CFF Cat Fanciers' Federation, Inc., a cat federation.

CONFORMATION The "look" or physical type of a cat, as measured against its breed standard.

CORONAVIRUS A family of related viruses.

DAM The mother of a cat.

DECLAW To have the claws from the paws of a cat permanently removed, usually by surgery. The only declawed cats that can be shown in cat shows are HHPs, and not every show or federation allows declawed HHPs to be shown.

DERMATITIS An inflammation of the skin.

ENTRY FORM The form used by a cat club that provides the information necessary for a cat to enter a cat show.

FADING KITTEN SYNDROME Apparently healthy newborn kittens lose vitality and die quickly (usually within the first 3 to 10 days of life) with no evidence of illness or congenital problems.

FANCY Short for "the Cat Fancy."

FERAL Wild or untamed.

FeLV Feline leukemia.

FIP Feline infectious peritonitis.

GENE POOL A term describing the genetic constitution of a group of individual cats.

GENETIC CODE A combination of letters and numbers designed to describe a cat in genetic terms. The purpose is to permit the cat to be classified properly for show and breeding purposes.

HHP Abbreviation for Household Pet (cat or kitten) in a cat show.

HOUSEHOLD PET A non-pedigreed cat or kitten or a pedigreed cat or kitten being exhibited in a class with non-pedigreed cats or kittens. Some cat federations have a separate procedure for registering HHPs. Some federations also permit household pets to earn titles equivalent to those won by pedigreed cats. Household pets are usually required to be altered by a certain age and may or may not be permitted to be declawed.

INBREEDING A breeding practice involving mating cats that are closely related to each other, such as first cousin matings, father to daughter, brother to sister, and offspring to grandparents. Inbreeding can be an undesirable practice, since breeding of closely related animals can accentuate existing genetic problems, even if they have not made themselves evident in past generations.

KITTEN A feline, of either sex, under the age of eight months.

For purposes of cat shows, a cat that is at least four months old, but less than eight months old. Its age is measured at the time of the show.

LINEBREEDING A form of inbreeding involving breeding individuals within the same bloodline. Cats within the same bloodline differ from each other in most generations; common ancestors are found further back in the breed's history.

LITTER All of the kittens born of the same sire and dam at the same time.

LITTER REGISTRATION The recording by a cat federation of the birth of a litter, giving the date of birth, number of kittens, as well as the sire and dam. Litter applications are submitted by the breeder of the litter.

NEUTER A male cat who has been castrated to prevent breeding.

NEUTERING Altering a male cat.

OUTCROSS Breeding one cat to another unrelated cat.

PAPERS One way to refer to a cat's certificate of registration and pedigree form.

PEDIGREE A document showing a cat's background for three, four, or five generations. A three-generation pedigree includes the present cat, plus three generations back. A pedigree gives names, colors, and registration numbers for each cat in the pedigree. Show titles are usually also given.

PEDIGREED CAT Usually refers to a cat whose heritage is known, documented, and registered.

POINTED A cat on which the mask (face), ears, legs, feet, and tail are clearly a darker shade, but that shade merges into the body color.

PREMIER In CFA, a class where altered cats are judged.

PYOMETRA An infection in the uterus.

QUEEN A breeding female cat.

REGISTERED CAT A cat (whether purebred or HHP) that has completed the requirements for registration with one of the cat federations.

REGISTRATION The initial recording of a cat's individual cat name/owner record in a cat federation. This also refers to the registration certificate issued by a cat federation to the registered owner of the cat.

REGISTRATION NUMBER A unique number assigned by a federation to identify one cat. Each federation issues its own set of registration numbers.

REGISTRATION RULES The rules and guidelines set up by a cat federation for the registration of cats, litters, catteries, etc.

REGISTRY One term used to describe a cat federation, taken from one of its primary roles, registering the birth and pedigree of cats.

RING A competition judged by one judge.

SHORTHAIR One of the two groups into which all cats are divided (long hair being the other).

SHOW CONFIRMATION A form used by a cat club confirming your cat's entry into a cat show.

SHOW FLYER A brochure that contains essential information about a cat show, including judges and fees.

SHOW RULES Rules formulated by a cat federation governing all the aspects of how that federation is to be managed.

SHOW A series of rings of judging sponsored by a cat club.

SIRE The father of a cat.

SPAY A female cat who has had a hysterectomy to prevent breeding and heat cycles.

SPAYING Altering a female cat.

SPECIALTY RING A ring where only cats of the same hair length (longhair or shorthair) are judged against each other.

SPRAYING A male cat's habit of urinating anywhere, probably associated with establishing territory. Sometimes a female cat will also spray.

STANDARDS OF PERFECTION Another name for breed standards, often just referred to as "standards."

STUD CAT A breeding male cat, also called a "working male."

TICA The International Cat Association, Inc., a cat federation.

TORTIE A shorthand way of describing a tortoiseshell cat, that is, one with black mingled with red.

TOXOPLASMOSIS An infection caused by an intracellular parasite. While it can be spread to humans, it is virtually non-existent in closed cat populations that are not allowed to hunt, or that are not fed raw or under cooked meat.

UPPER RESPIRATORY INFECTION (URI) Infection impacting the upper respiratory tract, characterized by signs such as sneezing, coughing, and nasal discharges.

VETTED SHOW A show where the cats are examined by a veterinarian either before they can be brought into the hall or before they are judged.

WHOLE MALE A male cat that has not been neutered.

Useful Addresses and Literature

United States Cat Registries

American Association of Cat Enthusiasts (AACE)
PO Box 213
Pine Brook, NJ 07058
(201) 335-6717

American Cat Association (ACA)
8101 Katherine Avenue
Panorama City, CA 91402
(818) 781-5656

American Cat Fanciers' Association (ACFA)
PO Box 203
Pt. Lookout, MO 65726
(417) 334-5430

Cat Fanciers' Association (CFA)
PO Box 1005
Manasquan, NJ 08736-0805
(908) 528-9797

Cat Fanciers' Federation (CFF)
PO Box 661
Gratis, OH 45330
(513) 787-9009

The International Cat Association (TICA)
PO Box 2684
Harlingen, TX 78551
(210) 428-8046

National Independent Breed Club

United Burmese Cat Fanciers
c/o Marianne Bolling
2395 N.E. 185th Street
North Miami, FL 33180

Cat Magazines

Cats
PO Box 290037
Port Orange, FL 32129-0037
(904) 788-2770

Cat Fancier's Almanac
The Cat Fanciers' Association, Inc.
PO Box 1005
Manasquan, NJ 08736-0805
(908) 528-9797

Cat Fancy/CatsUSA
PO Box 6050
Mission Viejo, CA 92690
(714) 855-8822

Cat World™ International
PO Box 35635
Phoenix, AZ 85069-5635
(602) 995-1822

I Love Cats
Grass Roots Publishing Company, Inc.
950 Third Avenue
New York, NY 10022-2705
(212) 888-1855

Books for Additional Reading

Behrend, Katrin. *Indoor Cats.* Barron's Educational Series, Inc., Hauppauge, NY: 1995.

Daly, Carol Himsel, D.V.M., *Caring for Your Sick Cat.* Barron's Educational Series, Inc., Hauppauge, NY: 1994.

Frye, Fredric. *First Aid for Your Cat.* Barron's Educational Series, Inc., Hauppauge, NY: 1987.

McGinnis, Terri, D.V.M. *The Well Cat Book.* Random House Books, New York: 1975.

McHattie, Grace. *Your Cat Naturally.* Carroll & Graf Publishers, Inc., New York:1992.

Pedersen, Niels C., D.V.M., Ph.D. *Feline Infectious Diseases.* American Veterinary Publications, Inc., Goleta, CA: 1988.

Stephens, Gloria. *Legacy of the Cat.* Chronicle Books, San Francisco, CA: 1990.

Vella, Carolyn M. and John J. McGonagle, Jr. *In the Spotlight: A Guide to Showing Pedigreed and Household Pet Cats.* Howell Book House, New York: 1990.

Viner, Bradley, D.V.M. *The Cat Care Manual.* Barron's Educational Series, Inc., Hauppauge, NY: 1993.

Wolff, H.G., D.V.M. *Your Healthy Cat.* North Atlantic Books, Berkeley, CA: 1991.

Index